KOOTEN
KI

MW01687354

presents...

a tasteful collection of Kootenay favorite recipes which have been originally created, or handed down within our families and friends; and beautiful landscape photos of the treasured Kootenay Country Region we can all be proud to share.

by
Sandy Smith

KOOTENAY COUNTRY KITCHENS COOKBOOK

---

by Sandy Smith

Second Printing Fall 2000

Published and Distributed by
Kootenay Kitchens Publishing
P.O. Box 656
Nakusp, British Columbia
Canada VOG 1R0

Canadian Cataloguing in Publication Data

Smith, Sandy, 1965-
Kootenay Country Kitchens Cookbook : a collection of Kootenay Favorites

Includes index.
ISBN 0-9682129-0-5

1.. Cookery, Canadian—British Columbia style.
2. Cookery— British Columbia—Kootenay Region.
I. Title

TX715.6.S585 1997 641.59711'62 C97-900458-6

Copyright © by Kootenay Kitchens Publishing
All Rights Reserved

Printed and bound in Canada by
Friesens, Altona, Manitoba

Acknowledgements

Dedicated to my husband Gerry and children Justine, Tyson and Kaitlyn for their time, patience and love. And to the rest of my family and friends who were very supportive and encouraging throughout this exciting venture.

My Thanks:

For all the tasteful recipes submitted by the people of the Kootenay Country who enjoy sharing wonderful, nutritional, easy to prepare and creative food ideas.

Test Kitchen: Kelley Buckley

Illustrations: Bobbi Urness

Food Stylist: Lyn Arikado

Food Photography: Bryan Anglin

Landscape Photography:
David Gluns - cover, pages 37, 55, 73, 109, 127
Larry Doell - pages 19, 91, 145

Front Cover:
Grouse and Wild Rice with Orange Sauce, page 78
A Kootenay Country Kitchens dish overlooking Slocan Lake and the Valhalla Range of the Selkirk Mountains.

TABLE OF CONTENTS

Kootenay Way Of Life

Sandy Smith
Publisher

Ever wonder how lucky we are to live the Kootenay lifestyle?

Mountain & lake views	3 cups	750 mL
Wildlife	1 cup	250 mL
Heritage	2 cups	500 mL
Outdoor adventure	2 cups	500 mL
Clean air	1 cup	250 mL
Natural hot springs	1 cup	250 mL
History	2 cups	500 mL
Nature	3 cups	750 mL
Warm weather	2 cups	500 mL

In ones lifetime, mix together all ingredients with peace, freedom and happiness. Flavor the mixture well with little gifts of love and kindness. Use 4 cups of community pride to enlighten the other ingredients and raise the texture of Kootenay living. Bake well with family and friends and serve with a smile.

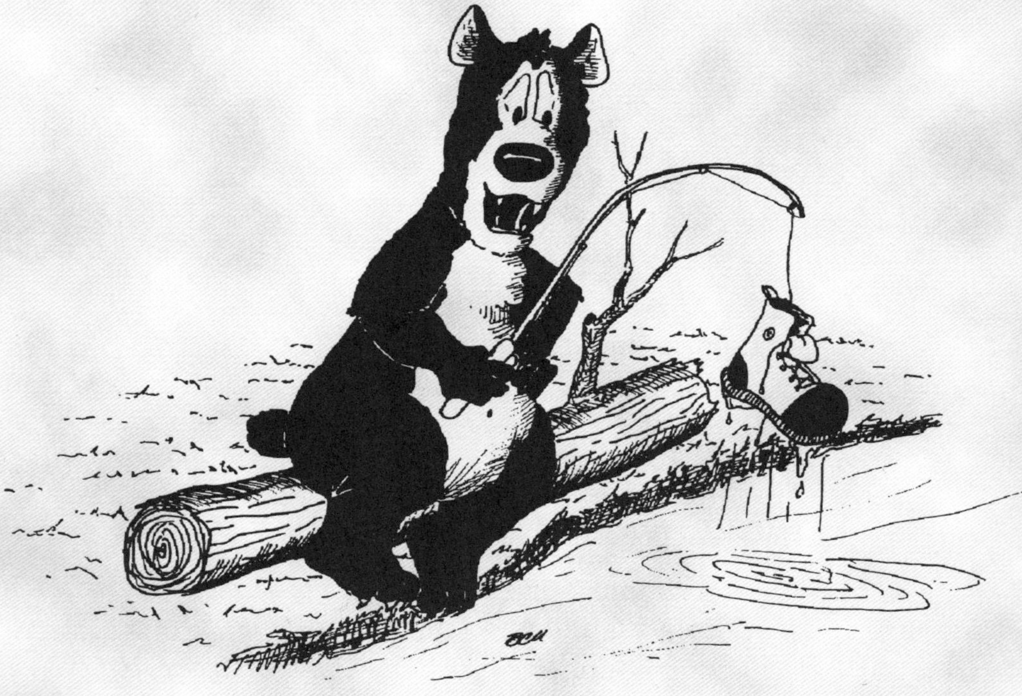

Seafood Nacho Dip

Marilyn & Eric Guillaume's Kitchen

A seafood dip is special no matter where you live, but it's extra special for Kootenay people!

Cream cheese	8 oz.	250 g
Salad dressing	1/2 cup	125 mL
Sour cream	1 cup	250 mL
Canned cocktail shrimp	6 oz.	170 g
Seafood sauce	10 oz.	283 g
Cheddar cheese, grated	1 cup	250 ml
Medium tomatoes, diced	2	2
Green onion, chopped	1/2 cup	125 mL

Mix the first 3 ingredients together in a bowl. Spread on bottom of 9 inch (23 cm) flat serving dish.

Layer cream cheese mixture with shrimp, seafood sauce, cheese diced tomatoes and onion. Serve with nacho chips or crackers.

Variation: You may substitute seafood sauce with same quantity of taco sauce.

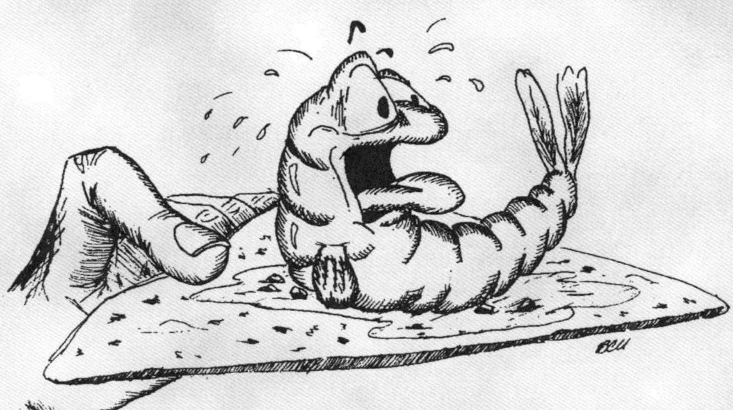

Antipasto

Lois Currie
Creston, BC

"Antipasto is a labour of love and any antipasto lover will know and appreciate this. Enjoy on crackers or on buns with cheese, placed under the broiler."

Cauliflower	2 lbs.	1 kg
Pickling onions (silver skins)	3 lbs.	1.5 kg
Red peppers	2 lbs.	1 kg
Green peppers	2 lbs.	1 kg
Dill pickles	1 quart	1 L
Canned green beans	3x 14 oz.	3x 398 mL
Pitted black olives	2x 14 oz.	2x 398 mL
Canned mushrooms pieces	2x 10 oz.	2x 284 mL
Stuffed green olives	2x 14 oz	2x 398 mL
Canned chunk tuna	4x 7 oz.	4x 198 g
Ketchup	10 cups	2.5 L
Oil	1/4 cup	60 mL
White vinegar	1/2 cup	125 mL

Chop all fresh vegetables to desired size.

Drain pickles, green beans, black olives, mushrooms and green olives. Drain and break up tuna.

Put ketchup, oil and vinegar in large pot. Add vegetables and tuna. Mix well. Bring to a boil, reduce heat and simmer about 15 minutes.

Put in sterilized jars. Carefully place jars in boiling water for 15 minutes to seal lids.

Health Crackers

Lyn Arikado
Nakusp, BC

Finally... a home-made nutritious cracker.

Rolled oats	3 cups	750 mL
Flour	2 cups	500 mL
Wheatgerm	1 cup	250 mL
Sugar	3 tbsp.	45 mL
Salt	1 tsp.	5 mL
Salad oil	$^{3}/_{4}$ cup	175 mL
Water	1 cup	250 mL
Egg white, slightly beaten	1	1
Sesame seeds (optional)		
Garlic OR onion salt (optional)		

Combine oats, flour, wheatgerm, sugar and salt in a bowl. Add water and oil. Stir until well mixed and dough forms.

Divide dough into quarters. Roll each quarter out on slightly floured surface to make 10 x 12 inch (25 x 30 cm) rectangle. Roll dough loosely around rolling pin and place on greased cookie sheet. Cut into squares or diamonds. Brush with beaten egg white. Sprinkle with sesame seeds, onion OR garlic salt. Bake in a 350°F (175°C) oven for 15-20 minutes, or until golden brown. Store in airtight container once well cooled.

Pictured on page 17.

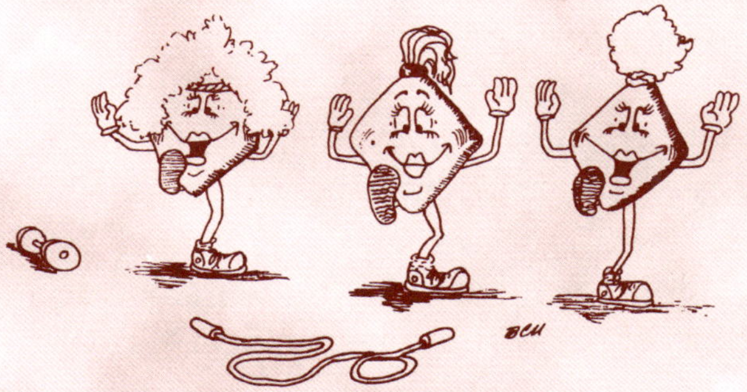

Macho Nacho Mexican Dip

Wade Buckley
Nakusp, BC

An all time favorite.

Refried beans	14 oz.	398 mL
Jalapeño peppers, finely chopped	2-3	2-3
Avocados, well mashed	3	3
Lemon juice	2 tbsp.	30 mL
Pepper	1/4 tsp.	1 mL
Salt	1/2 tsp.	2 mL
Mayonnaise	1/2 cup	125 mL
Sour cream	1 cup	250 mL
Package of taco mix	1	1
Green onions, chopped	6	6
Medium tomatoes, seedless and chopped	3	3
Pitted black olives, chopped	14 oz.	398 mL
Sharp OR mozzarella cheese, grated	8 oz.	250 g

Mix together refried beans, jalapeño peppers. Spread on bottom of 10 inch (25 cm) deep pie dish.

In a bowl, combine avocados, lemon juice, pepper and salt. Spread on bean mixture.

Mix mayonnaise, sour cream and taco mix together in bowl. Spread on as third layer in pie dish.

Add all the remaining ingredients one at a time following layering pattern. Serve with tortilla chips.

Nutty Nutballs

Kim Fuzzen
Crawford Bay, BC

You must start 4-8 hours prior to enjoying this unique appetizer, for the nuts require presoaking.

Walnuts, soaked	1 cup	250 mL
Sunflower seeds, soaked	1 cup	250 mL
Sprouted buckwheat	2 cups	500 mL
Honey	3 tbsp.	45 mL
Nutmeg, dash		

ORANGE SAUCE:

Concentrated orange juice, thawed	12 oz.	341 mL
Water	1 1/2 cups	375 mL
Honey	2-3 tbsp.	30-45 mL
Flour	1 tsp.	5 mL
Nutmeg, dash		

Grind first 3 ingredients together. Stir in honey and nutmeg. Form dough into one inch (2.5 cm) balls. Fry in oil, or bake in 325°F (160°C) oven for 6-8 minutes or till lightly browned. Pour orange sauce on nut balls and enjoy. Makes 2 1/2 dozen.

Orange sauce:
In a saucepan, combine orange juice, water, honey, flour and nutmeg. Stir and heat on stove until sauce thickens.

To soak nuts: Cover with water and let stand 4-8 hours. Drain before using.

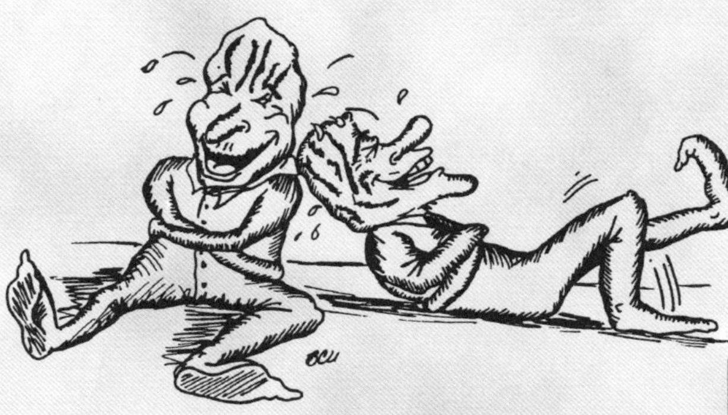

Pumpernickel Loaf

Barb Williams' and Cris Dawson's Kitchen
North Shore
Nelson, BC

A popular appetizer among friends.

Bacon	1 lb.	500 g
Onion, finely chopped	1 cup	250 mL
Frozen spinach (thawed, drained and chopped)	10 oz.	284 g
Old Cheddar cheese, grated	1 cup	250 mL
Garlic cloves, crushed	2	2
Cream cheese, softened	2x 8 oz.	2x 250 g
Mayonnaise	1 cup	250 mL
Seasoned salt, to taste		
Whole pumpernickel OR sourdough bread	1	1

In a skillet, fry bacon until crispy. Crumble and put in bowl.

Add remaining 7 ingredients and mix thoroughly. Set aside.

The bread will become the serving bowl. Slice a lid on top of the bread and hollow the center. Reserve the bread cubes. Fill the hollow loaf with the cream cheese mixture and replace the lid. Wrap the loaf well with tin foil and bake in 325°F (160°C) oven for 2 hours. Serve as dip for reserved bread cubes and crackers.

Remove the tin foil and serve as a hot dip with bread cubes, crackers and veggies. You can even eat the bowl!

Quesadillas
(Mexican Grilled Cheese Sandwich)

The Villanueva Family
Nakusp, BC

"Mexican food has experienced great increased popularity for the last 20 years, and is topped only by Chinese cuisine as top ethnic foods enjoyed by Canadians. As most Canadians, people living in the KOOTENAYS prefer more meat and cheese in their food than their Mexican Amigos. This recipe also takes into consideration the busy Canadian lifestyle, and lack of ethnic spices."

Vegetable oil
Soft tortillas
Cheddar, Jack, or Marble cheese, grated

SUGGESTIONS:
Chopped tomatoes
Chopped green peppers
Chopped jalapeño peppers
Chopped onions
Sliced mushrooms
Refried beans
Chopped ham
Any cooked or smoked meat of your choice

Salsa, optional
Sour cream, optional

Heat oil in hot skillet. Place tortilla in skillet and add cheese with any other fillings. Place another tortilla on top. Grill on both sides till cheese is melted. Cut into wedges.

Another option for cooking is to microwave for 45 seconds on high. Ideal with soup, salad or as a light snack.

Pictured on page 17.

Garlic Spread

Lyn Arikado
Nakusp, BC

This spread is wonderful with health crackers on page 9 or tortilla crackers on page 15. It keeps for days in the refrigerator.

Cream cheese	8 oz.	250 g
Mayonnaise	1 cup	250 g
Sour cream	1 cup	250 g
Garlic cloves, crushed	4	4
Paprika	1/2 tsp.	2 mL

Whip all the ingredients together until smooth. Refrigerate until ready to serve.

Pictured on page 17.

Hot Artichoke Spread

Beth Guillaume
Trail, BC

Artichoke "heart" is the prized section of an artichoke.

Artichoke hearts (drained and chopped)	14 oz.	398 mL
Grated parmesan cheese	1/2 cup	125 mL
Mayonnaise	1/2 cup	125 mL
Garlic salt	1/2 tsp.	2 mL
Lemon juice	1/2-1 tsp.	2-5 mL

Mix all ingredients together in a bowl. Transfer into flat serving dish. Bake in 350°F (175°C) oven for 10-15 minutes. Excellent with crackers.

Pictured on page 17.

Tortilla Crackers

Lyn Arikado
Nakusp, BC

Great served with garlic spread and Jalapeño or red pepper jellies. Or, try salsa or antipasto. Warning: When you start eating these, you can't stop.

Flour tortilla shells, 10 inch	16-24	16-24
Butter OR margarine, melted	1/4 cup	60 mL
Olive oil	1/4 cup	60 mL
Garlic salt	1 tsp.	5 mL
Basil	1/2 tsp.	2 mL
Coriander	1/2 tsp.	2 mL
Dried oregano	1 tsp.	5 mL
Cumin	1/2 tsp.	2 mL
Parsley	1 tbsp.	15 mL

Cut tortilla shells into wedges. Set aside.

Mix remaining 8 ingredients together in large bowl. Add tortilla shells and toss until lightly glazed.

Lay wedges flat on baking sheets and bake in 425°F (220°C) oven for 8-10 minutes, until lightly browned. Cool on cooling rack. Good hot or cold. When cooled, store in airtight container.

Suggested serving: Two to three 10 inch (25 cm) shells per person.

Pictured on page 17.

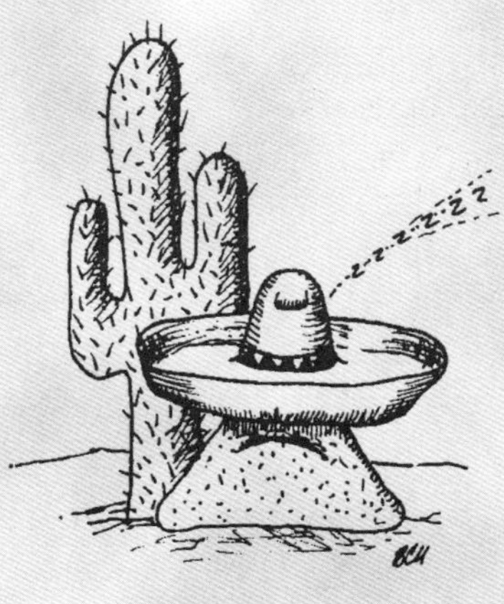

Salmon Balls - Salmonettes

Lynn Howard
Pilot Bay Resort
Kootenay Bay, BC

"Very good with seafood sauce".

Canned salmon	2x 7 1/2 oz.	2x 213 g
Egg	1	1
Flour	1/2 cup	125 mL
Pepper, to taste		
Baking powder	1 tsp.	5 mL

Drain salmon, reserving juice. Put salmon in bowl and add egg, flour and pepper. Mix well.

In a separate bowl, mix baking powder and reserved salmon juice. This mixture should foam or the baking powder is stale and will not work. Pour into salmon and egg mixture and mix well.

Drop small balls in hot fat. They should expand and rise to the top. Drain on paper towel and serve hot with several dips of your choice.

Hot Artichoke Spread, page 14
Tortilla Crackers, page 15
Health Crackers, page 9
Quesadillas, page 13
Salsa Roja, page 19
Garlic Spread, page 14
Jalapeño Pepper Jelly, page 150
Sweet Pepper Jelly, page 151

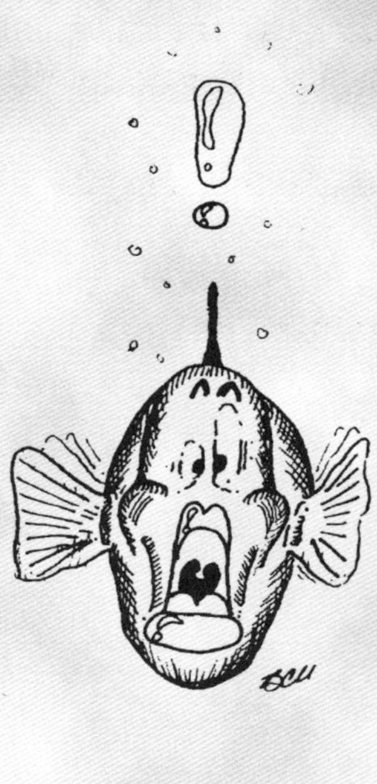

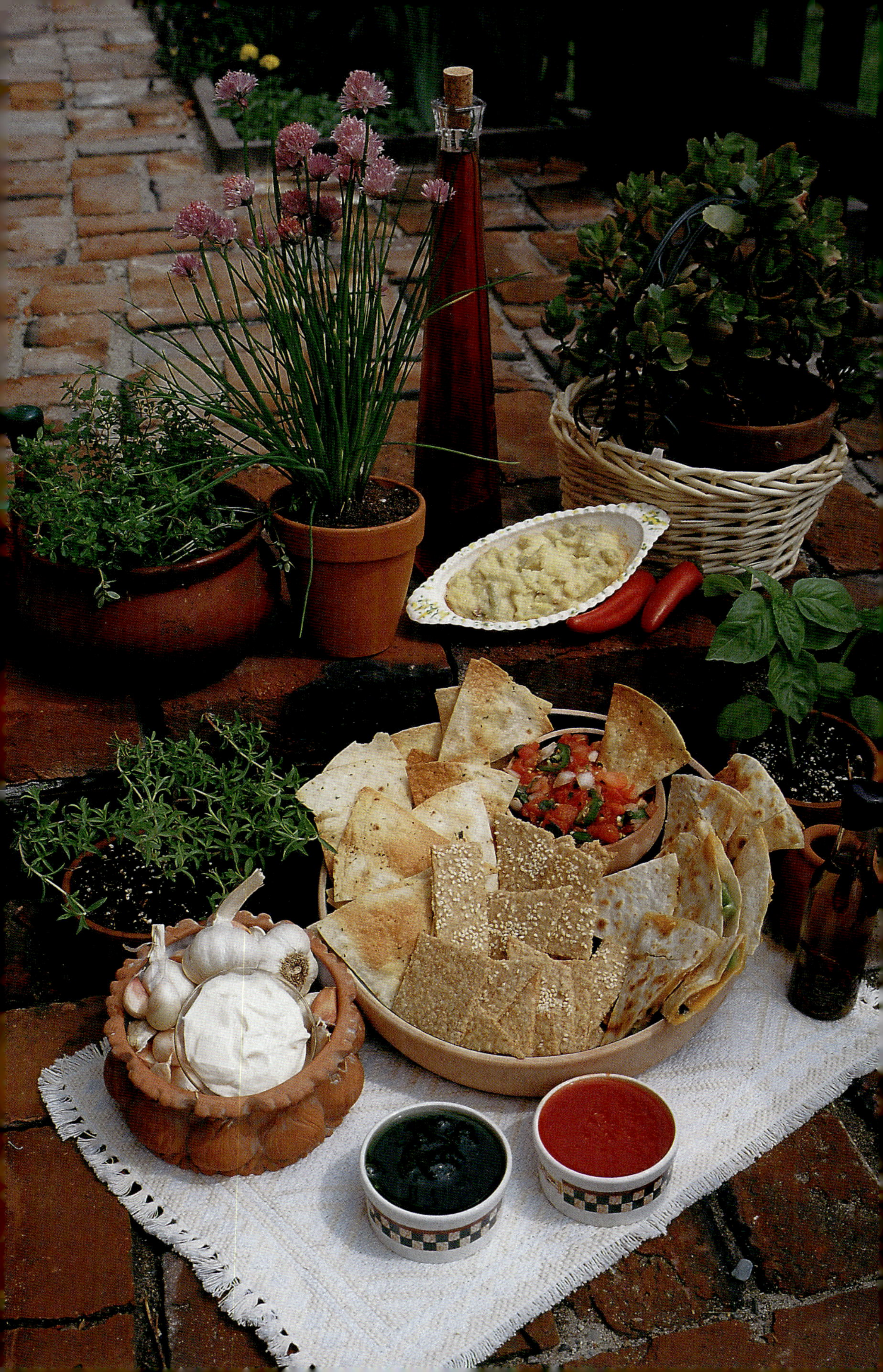

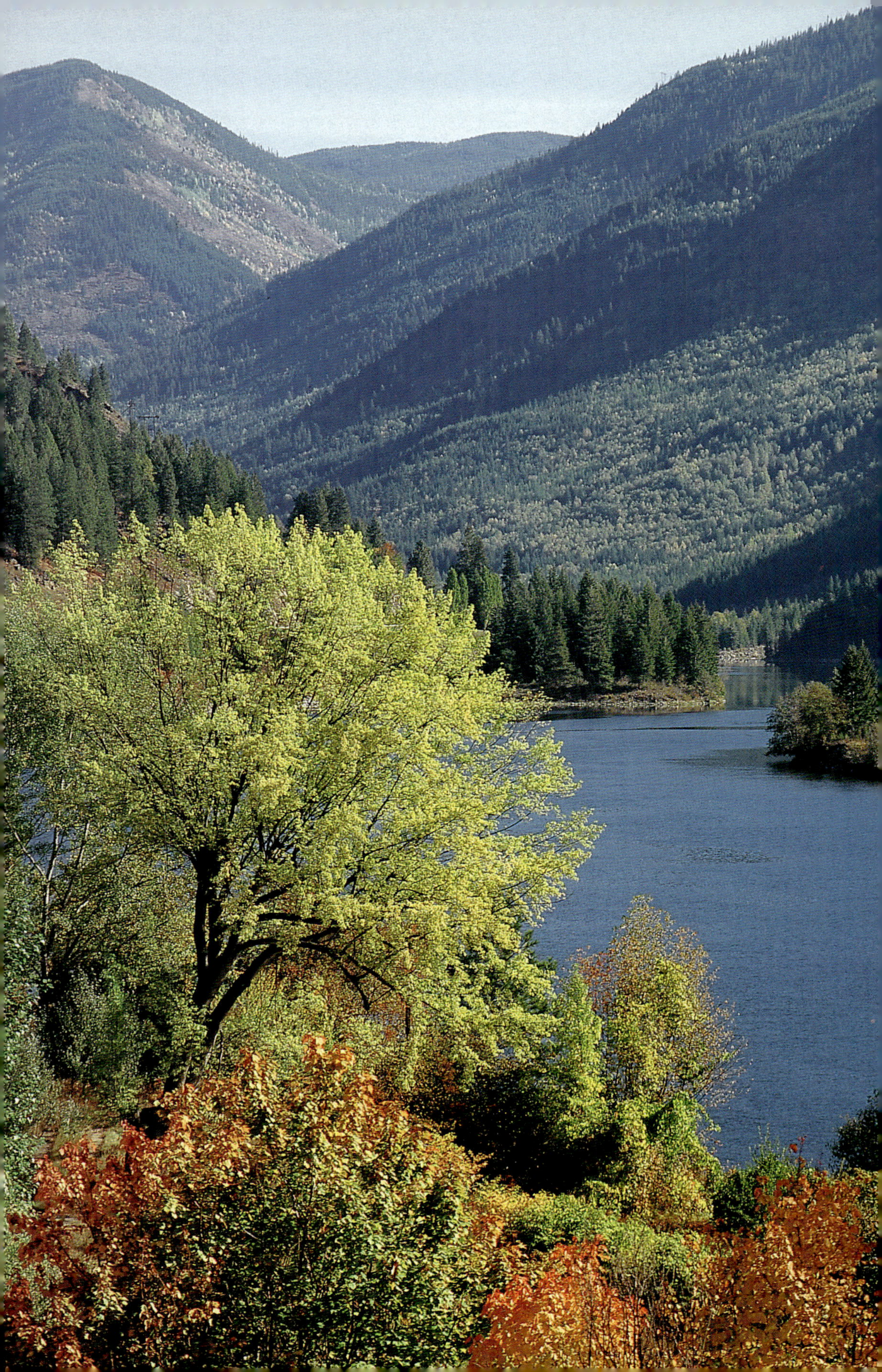

Salsa Roja (Red Salsa)

The Villanueva Family
Nakusp, BC

"Be sure to invite all your amigos to try this salsa."

Tomatoes, diced (fresh or canned)	14 oz.	398 mL
White onion, diced	1/4 cup	60 mL
Jalapeño or serrano peppers, diced	4-6	4-6
Salt	1/4 tsp.	1 mL
Oregano	1/8 tsp.	0.5 mL
Garlic powder	1/8 tsp.	0.5 mL
Cilantro, diced (optional)	1 tsp.	5 mL

Mix all ingredients in a glass bowl. Cover and refrigerate for at least 1 hour.

As this salsa is fresh, and the ingredients are mostly acidic, it is only good for a day or two.

Salud

Pictured on page 17.

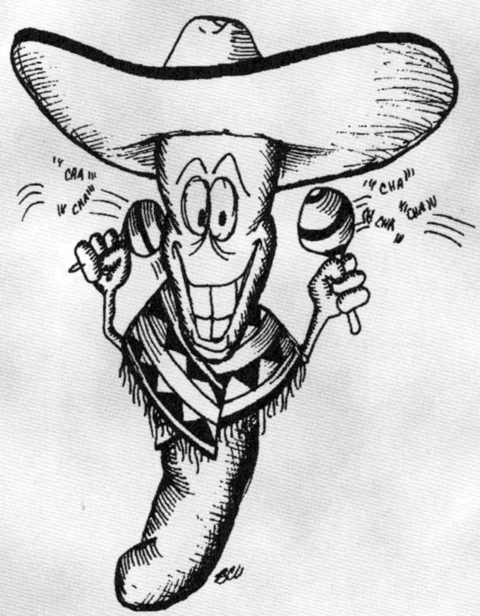

Serene beauty of the Kootenay River near Castlegar.

Scallops and Wild Mushrooms

Geoff Hampson
Mountain Gypsy Cafe
Rossland, BC

A wonderful dish with your favorite wild mushrooms.

Wild mushrooms (chanterelle, pine, oyster, OR shitake)	1/3 cup	100 g
Butter	2 tbsp.	30 mL
Garlic clove, chopped	1	1
Sea scallops	20	20
Sake	1/4 tsp.	1 mL
Light soy sauce	1 tbsp.	15 mL
Butter	1 1/2 oz.	40 g
Small red pepper, finely sliced	1	1
Small green pepper, finely sliced	1	1
Small yellow pepper, finely sliced	1	1
Black pepper, pinch		

In a skillet, sauté sliced mushrooms in butter until soft.

Add garlic and scallops to skillet. Cook over medium heat until scallops are tender, approximately 2 minutes. Add sake and cook over high heat for approximately 1/2 minute. Mix in soy sauce, butter, peppers and black pepper. Swirl pan until butter melts and binds. Serve immediately. Makes 2 servings.

DID YOU KNOW... The ever popular "Pine", "Chanterelle", "Oyster", "Shaggy Mane", "Giant Puff Balls", "Gypsy", "Morel", "Honey", and "Meadow" are only a few of the wild mushrooms that grow in the Kootenay Country.

Soothing Smoothie

Hazel Calder
New Denver, BC

"A healthy refreshing fruity beverage your children will love. Especially delicious for pregnant ladies."

Fruits of choice (apple, strawberry, papaya, green grapes, peach, pear, banana)	3	3
Orange OR pear juice	1 cup	250 mL
Plain yogurt	1/2 cup	125 mL
Ice cubes	3	3

Mix together 3 fruit choices, juice, yogurt and ice in blender. Blend until well mixed and serve. Makes 2-4 servings.

Variation: Substitute yogurt with 1/2 cup (125 mL) buttermilk.

Pictured on page 71.

Banana Wheat Germ Shake

One portion of fruit, two portions of dairy, one portion of grain with an added touch of sweetness. Once assembled, it's one well balanced powerful drink!

Milk	2 cups	500 mL
Large banana	1	1
Egg	1	1
Honey	1 tbsp.	15 mL
Wheat germ	1 tbsp.	15 mL

Combine all ingredients in blender. Blend until evenly mixed. Enjoy! Makes 2 servings.

Summer Iced Tea

Dreana Ratcliffe
Nakusp, BC

Experiment with a variety of different tea bags for extra fun and flavor.

Tea bags	5-6	5-6
Cold water	16 cups	4 L
Sugar	1 cup	250 mL
Lemon juice	3/4 cup	175 mL

Place tea bags into large gallon sized jug. Add water. Set in sun for 8 hours.

Remove tea bags. Stir in sugar and lemon juice. Chill and enjoy. Serves 16 thirsty people.

Pictured on page 35.

Creamy Irish Cream

Lyn Arikado
Nakusp, BC

A nice after dinner addition to your coffee.

Rye OR Irish whiskey	1 1/2 cups	375 mL
Sweetened condensed milk	11 oz.	300 mL
Whipping cream	2 cups	500 mL
Egg	1	1
Almond extract	1/2 tsp.	2 mL
Chocolate syrup	3 tbsp.	45 mL
Instant coffee	1 tsp.	5 mL

Put all ingredients in bowl or blender and slow whip for 2-3 minutes. Pour into desired jars or containers. Refrigerate.

Cheesy Corn Chowder

Peggy Tugwell
Crawford Bay, BC

The long growing climate in the Kootenays allows abundance of fresh garden vegetables.

Boiling water OR stock	2 1/2 cups	625 mL
Potatoes, diced	2 cups	500 mL
Carrots, diced	1/2 cup	125 mL
Celery, diced	1/2 cup	125 mL
Onions, diced	1/2 cup	125 mL
Red pepper, diced	1/2 cup	125 mL
Salt	1 tsp.	5 mL
Butter OR margarine	1/4 cup	60 mL
Flour	1/4 cup	60 mL
Milk	2 cups	500 mL
Sharp Cheddar cheese, grated	1 cup	250 mL
Corn (fresh, canned OR frozen)	2 cups	500 mL

In a large saucepan, bring first 7 ingredients to a boil. Reduce heat and simmer 15-20 minutes.

Melt butter in a heavy pot. Stir in flour. Simmer one minute, stirring constantly. Add milk and whisk until thickened. Stir in cheese until melted. Mix in corn and cooked vegetables with liquid. Heat but do not boil. Serve with fresh buns. Makes 4-6 servings.

Pictured on page 89.

New England Clam Chowder

Kay Ryan
Nelson, BC

Maybe this soup should be named "Kootenay Clam Chowder".

Salt pork, diced (rind removed)	1/2 lb.	230 g
Large onion, finely chopped	1	1
Boiling water	1 cup	250 mL
Medium potatoes, diced	3	3
Salt and pepper, to taste		
Thyme, to taste		
Minced baby clams	2x 5 oz.	2x 142 g
Milk	1 cup	250 mL
Light cream	2 cups	500 mL

Fry salt pork in skillet until brown and crisp. Remove pork from skillet and set aside.

In same skillet, sauté onion in remaining fat until lightly browned.

In a large pot add water, potatoes, salt, pepper and thyme. Cover and simmer until potatoes are tender, about 30 minutes.

Add clams with liquid to the pot, and heat. Stir in milk, cream and sautéed onions. Simmer until ready to serve. DO NOT BOIL. Serve in bowls topped with salt pork and additional thyme if desired. Makes 6 servings.

Note: When storing in the refrigerator, do not mix salt pork with soup when storing. The soup will become too salty.

Marvelous Mushroom Soup

Jenny Shkurhan
Wynndel, BC

"A sturdy egg slicer reduces the tedium of slicing all those mushrooms."

Small onion, chopped	1	1
Butter OR margarine	2 tbsp.	30 mL
Flour	3 tbsp.	45 mL
Oregano, dried	1/4 tsp.	1 mL
Pepper	1/2 tsp.	2 mL
Bay leaf	1	1
Water	1 cup	250 mL
Chicken broth	3x 10 oz.	3x 284 mL
Fresh mushrooms, sliced	1 lb.	500 g
Whipping cream OR light cream	1/2 cup	125 mL

In a large saucepan, sauté onion in butter until transparent. Stir in flour and seasonings. Slowly add water and broth, stirring constantly until thickened. Add mushrooms, cover and simmer for 30 minutes.

Stir in cream. Remove bay leaf and serve. Serves 4-6.

DID YOU KNOW... An active outbreak of summer thunderstorms may produce up to 1000 lightening strikes in a day throughout the Kootenay Country region.

Borscht in Dutch Oven

Diane Kalesnikoff
Thrums, BC

"This tasty borscht is of Doukhobor origin. It is a meatless soup because historically, the Doukhobors were vegetarians."

Finely chopped onions	1/2 cup	125 mL
Butter	1/4 cup	60 mL
Small beet, grated	1	1
Tomatoes, mashed	32 oz.	1 L
Boiling water	10 cups	2.4 L
Butter	1/4 cup	60 mL
Whipping cream	1/2 cup	125 mL
Salt	1 1/2 tbsp.	22 mL
Finely chopped onion	1/2 cup	125 mL
Potatoes, quartered	2 cups	500 mL
Finely diced carrots	2 cups	500 mL
Onion, finely chopped	2 cups	500 mL
Cabbage, finely chopped	4 cups	1 L
Butter	1/4 cup	60 mL
Butter	1/4 cup	60 mL
Whipping cream OR fresh cream (not half & half as it curdles)	3/4 cup	175 mL
Small green pepper, finely diced	1	1
Potatoes, cubed	2 cups	500 mL
Cabbage, shredded	1 1/2 cups	375 mL
Green onions, chopped	1 cup	250 mL
Finely chopped dill, fresh	1/2 cup	125 mL
OR dried dill	4 tbsp.	60 mL
Pepper, to taste		
Cayenne pepper, to taste		

Borscht in Dutch Oven
Continued...

When making this delicious Borscht, follow the steps and ingredients in the order as they are listed.

In a dutch oven (large heavy pot), sauté onions in butter. Add beet and tomatoes. Let simmer 15 to 20 minutes.

Add water, butter, whipping cream, salt, onion, potatoes, and carrots. Boil till the potatoes are tender.

Meanwhile in a skillet sauté onions and cabbage in butter until vegetables are transparent. Set aside.

Remove potatoes from dutch oven and put in a bowl. Mash in butter and whipping cream. Set aside.

Add green pepper and potatoes to Dutch oven. Boil for 2 minutes.

Stir in 1 cup Borscht juice into mashed potatoes and add to the dutch oven.

Add fresh cabbage to dutch oven and bring to a boil.

Add fried cabbage mixture to dutch oven and bring to another boil. Remove from stove. Stir in green onions and dill. Sprinkle black pepper, and cayenne pepper on top and serve. Store in fridge after it cools.

Storage idea: This soup may be stored in the fridge for up to 2 months. Seal by putting the hot Borscht into hot sterilized jars. While jars are hot, fill with Borscht, put on hot lids and seal. Let cool and keep in fridge.

Pictured on page 89.

Hamburger Soup

Judy Hunter
Nelson, BC

Four soup choices. Try all of them and struggle to pick a favorite.

Lean hamburger	1 1/2 lbs.	750 g
Water	2 cups	500 mL
Carrots, grated OR chopped	4	4
Tomato soup	10 oz.	284 mL
Consommé	3x 10 oz.	3x 284 mL
Barley	1/2 cup	125 mL
Celery stalks, chopped	3-4	3-4
Tomatoes	28 oz.	796 mL
Parsley, sprinkle		
Thyme, sprinkle		
Salt and pepper, to taste		
Medium onion, chopped	1	1

Brown hamburger in a large pot. Stir in next 10 ingredients. Bring to a boil, reduce heat and simmer for 1 1/2 hours.

Add onion and simmer for another 30 minutes. Serves 6.

Variations:
For Mexican flavor - substitute barley for soaked beans. Use cumin chili powder, garlic powder and coriander instead of thyme.
For Oriental flavor - substitute barley for rice. Leave out thyme and tomato soup. Add 2 tbsp. (30 mL) soya sauce and one 10 oz. (284 mL) can sliced mushrooms with juice.
For Italian flavor - substitute barley for pasta. Use tomato paste instead of tomato soup. Use oregano, garlic powder and basil instead of thyme.

Beef & Barley Soup

Serve with Mark's Whole Wheat Bread on page 95 for a delicious nutritional meal.

Oil	1 tbsp.	15 mL
Stewing beef, 1" (2.5 cm) cubes	1 lb.	500 g
Water	8 cups	2 L
Beef bouillon cubes	2	2
Hot water	1/2 cup	125 mL
Canned tomatoes	14 oz.	398 mL
Carrots, diced	1 cup	250 mL
Onion, chopped	1 cup	250 mL
Celery, diced	1 cup	250 mL
Barley	1/2 cup	125 mL
Parsley, finely chopped	1/4 cup	60 mL
Salt	1/2 tsp.	2 mL
Pepper	1 1/2 tsp.	7 mL

Heat oil in a large pot. Add beef, stirring often until browned. Add water. Reduce heat, cover and simmer for 1 hour or until beef is tender.

Dissolve beef cubes in hot water. Pour in pot and add remaining ingredients. Cover and simmer 1 1/2-2 hours or until vegetables are tender. Makes 8 servings.

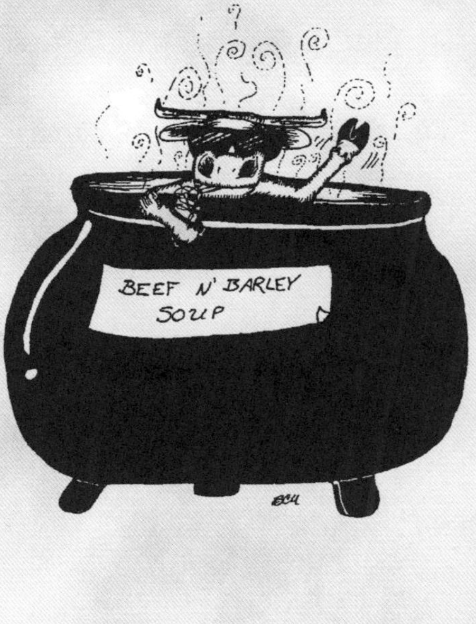

Bean & Noodle Break-up Soup

Kathy Dupuis
Nakusp, BC

"This recipe is a favorite of mine because not only is it tasty and nutritious - but it's also economical. Prime consideration when the logging roads 'break-up' and the boys are laid-off!"

Carrots, chopped	2	2
Medium onion, chopped	1	1
Zucchini, sliced	1	1
Green cabbage, shredded	1 1/2 cups	375 mL
Celery, chopped	1/2 cup	125 mL
Vegetable oil	2 tbsp.	30 mL
Vegetable OR chicken broth	4-6 cups	1-1.5 L
Combination of pepper, coriander, paprika, cayenne, allspice, bay leaf, cumin	1-2 tsp.	5-10 mL
Kidney, pinto OR romano beans (soaked OR rinsed canned)	1-2 cups	250-500 mL
		250 mL
Uncooked macaroni	1 cup	

In heavy pot, sauté vegetables in oil for 3 minutes.

Stir in broth and seasonings. Bring to a boil. Add beans and pasta, cover and simmer over low heat for 10 minutes or until pasta is tender. Stir occasionally. Serves 4-6.

Vegetable Bacon Chowder

Kathy Mackenzie
Nakusp, BC

For additional flavor and presentation, garnish with fresh chives or basil.

Bacon slices	10	10
Butter OR margarine	1 tbsp.	15 mL
Onion, chopped	2 cups	500 mL
Garlic cloves, minced	6	6
Salt	2 tsp.	10 mL
Thyme	1/2 tsp.	2 mL
Basil	2 tsp.	10 mL
Medium potato, diced	1	1
Celery stalks, diced	2	2
Carrots, diced	2	2
Broccoli, chopped	2 cups	500 mL
Cauliflower, small flowerets	2 cups	500 mL
Fresh mushrooms, chopped	1/2 lb.	250 g
Corn	2 cups	500 mL
Black pepper, to taste		
Water	1 1/2 cups	375 mL
Milk, hot	4 cups	1 L

In a skillet, cook bacon until crisp. Drain and crumble.

Melt butter in large pot. Add onion, half of garlic, salt, thyme and basil. Sauté on medium heat for 5 minutes. Mix in potato, celery, carrots, broccoli and cauliflower. Sauté for another 5-8 minutes.

Stir in mushrooms, corn and pepper and cook for 8-10 minutes. Add water and cover. Simmer for 1-5 minutes until tender. Stir in hot milk and remaining garlic. Remove from heat and add bacon. Serve with grated cheese on top. Makes 4-6 servings.

Marinated Tomatoes

Hazel Calder
New Denver, BC

A terrific salad for those garden fresh tomatoes.

Sliced tomatoes	2 cups	500 mL
MARINADE:		
Salad oil	1/2 cup	125 mL
Red wine vinegar	1/2 cup	125 mL
Celery, chopped	1/4 cup	60 mL
Green onion	1/4 cup	60 mL
Sugar	1 tsp.	5 mL
Dry mustard	1/2 tsp.	2 mL
Garlic cloves, crushed	2	2
Fresh chopped basil	2 tsp.	10 mL

Arrange tomatoes in low glass dish.

Put marinade ingredients in jar with lid. Blend by shaking. Pour over tomatoes, cover and chill. Serves 4-6.

Variation: Use 1/2 tsp. (2 mL) dried basil instead of fresh chopped basil.

Pictured on page 71.

DID YOU KNOW... Keeping tomatoes in storage with stems pointed downward will retain their freshness longer.

Milward's Caesar Salad

Russell
Crawford Bay, BC

DRESSING:		
Egg yolks	2	2
Olive oil	1/4 cup	60 mL
Garlic cloves, crushed	6	6
Dry mustard	1/2 tsp.	2 mL
Salt	1/2 tsp.	2 mL
Pepper	1/2 tsp.	2 mL
Anchovy fillet, finely chopped (optional)	1	1
Worcestershire sauce	1 tsp.	5 mL
Red wine vinegar	2 tbsp.	30 mL
Lemon juice	2 tbsp.	30 mL
Grated parmesan cheese	1/4 cup	60 mL
CROUTONS:		
Garlic cloves, crushed	3	3
Olive oil	1/4 cup	60 mL
Sourdough bread slices, cubed	10	10
Bunches romaine lettuce, torn in bite sized pieces	2	2

In a bowl, beat together egg yolks and olive oil until creamy. Mix in remaining 9 dressing ingredients. Blend well. Refrigerate.

In a large skillet, sauté garlic cloves in olive oil on medium heat. Reduce heat and mix in bread cubes. Stir until crunchy.

Put romaine lettuce into large salad bowl. Refrigerate. When ready to serve, toss with dressing. Add croutons and enjoy! Serves 10-12.

Gingered Cucumber

Gordon Brown
Kaslo, BC

Fresh ginger can elevate an ordinary dish into something really delicious.

Cucumbers	2	2
Salt	1 tsp.	5 mL
White vinegar	1/4 cup	60 mL
Sugar	1 1/2 tbsp.	22 mL
Fresh ginger, grated	1 tsp.	5 mL

Peel cucumbers close to skin. Run fork down lengthwise over cut surface to give fluted effect when sliced. In a bowl, cut cucumbers into thin slices. Sprinkle with salt. Mix well. Let stand 30 minutes.

Drain off excess liquid in bowl. Combine remaining ingredients and add to cucumber. Mix well. Refrigerate several hours before serving. Serves 4.

Sui Choy Salad, page 42
Cottage Stuffed Tomatoes, page 40
Pesto Tortellini Salad, page 44
Garlic Toast, page 93
Summer Iced Tea, page 22
Sue's Fruit Vinegar Dressing, page 38

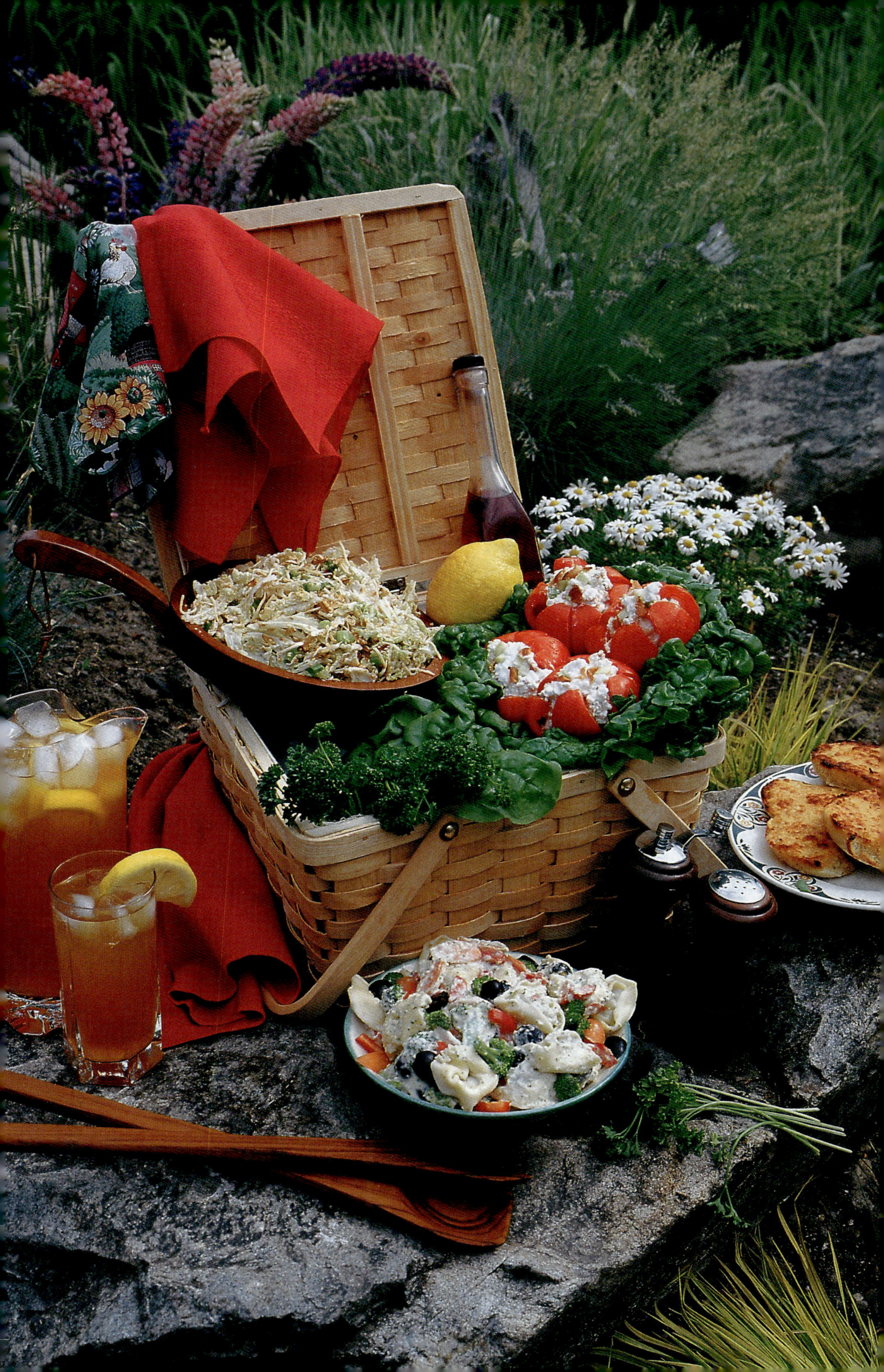

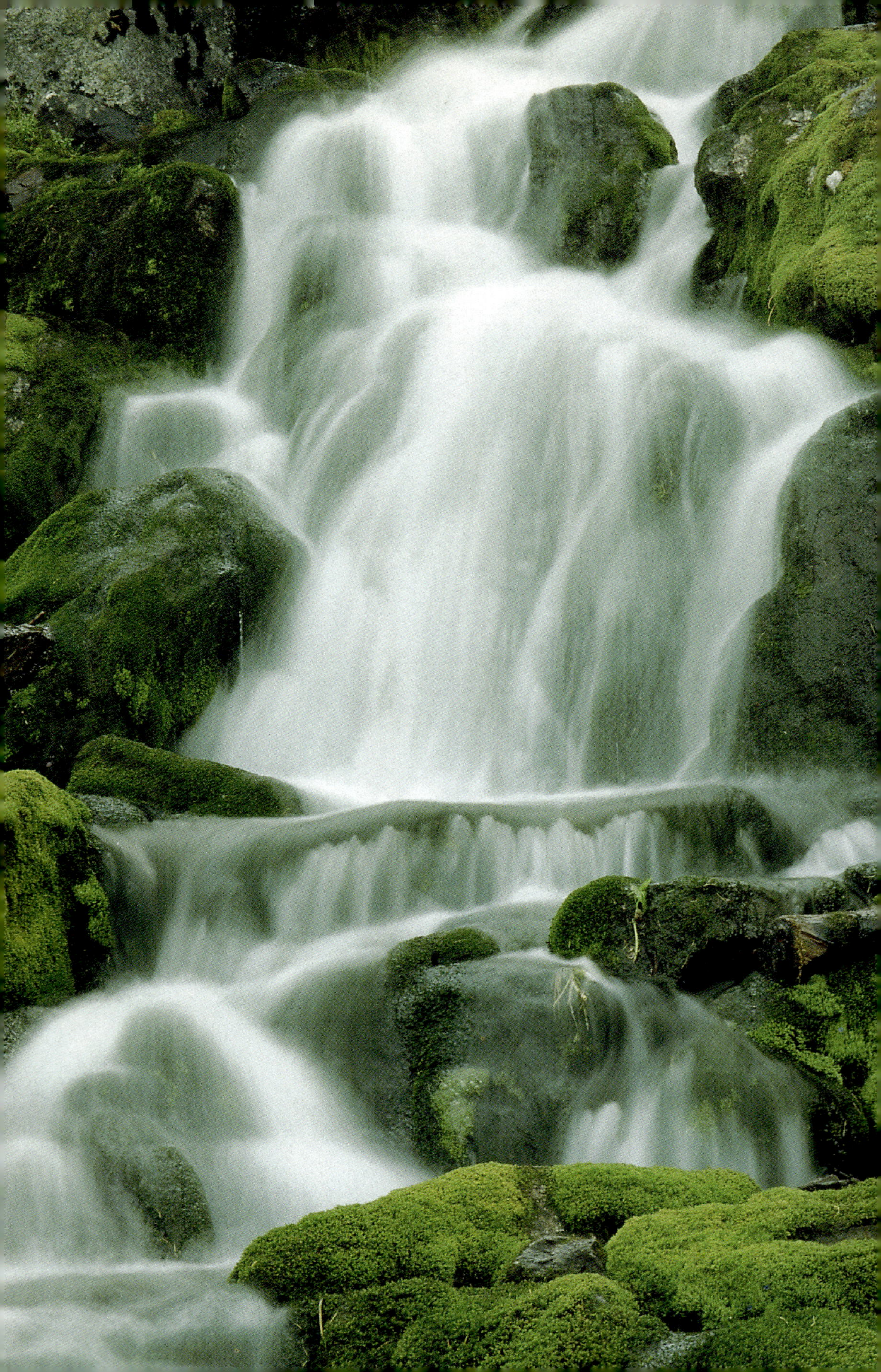

Oil & Vinegar Dressing

Anna G. Betnaza
Trail, BC

A dressing to your liking. Serve on favorite salad. This dressing is both affordable and nourishing as indicated in Anna's book 'Eat Anna's Way".

Apple cider vinegar	1/2 cup	125 mL
Olive oil	1 1/2 cups	375 mL
Sea salt	1/2 tsp.	2 mL
ANY OF THE FOLLOWING:		
Garlic cloves	1-2	1-2
Green onion stalks	2-3	2-3
Horse radish root (inch)	1	1
Parsley sprigs	3	3
Small cucumber	1	1
Dill	1 tsp.	5 mL
Small avocado	1/2	1/2
Dry mustard	1/2 tsp.	2 mL
Paprika	1/2 tsp.	2 mL

In a blender combine cider vinegar, olive oil and sea salt.

Add desired herbs and vegetables. Mix until all ingredients are well blended.

DID YOU KNOW... The Leland Hotel in Nakusp built in 1892 is reputed by some to be the oldest continuously operated hotel of its kind in British Columbia.

One of many waterfalls to be discovered in the Kootenays.

Sue's Fruit Vinegar Dressing

Kelley Buckley
Nakusp, BC

"This dressing is given to me as a Christmas present from my sister-in-law every year. I anxiously await each year to try a new flavor out. It's my favorite dressing."

Cider Vinegar	4 cups	1 L
Fresh OR frozen fruit (raspberries, cranberries, blueberries, strawberries, OR huckleberries)	1 cup	250 mL
Juice of an orange	1/4 cup	60 mL
Honey	1/4-1/2 cup	60-125 mL

Cloves/cinnamon sticks, (optional)

In a saucepan, bring first 4 ingredients to a boil. Reduce heat and simmer 2 minutes. Remove from heat and strain to discard berry pulp. Divide into vinegar bottles. In each bottle, put in few chosen fruit, cloves and cinnamon sticks.

To serve: Add equal amounts of this vinegar to equal amounts of oil. Shake well and serve over salad.

Pictured on page 35.

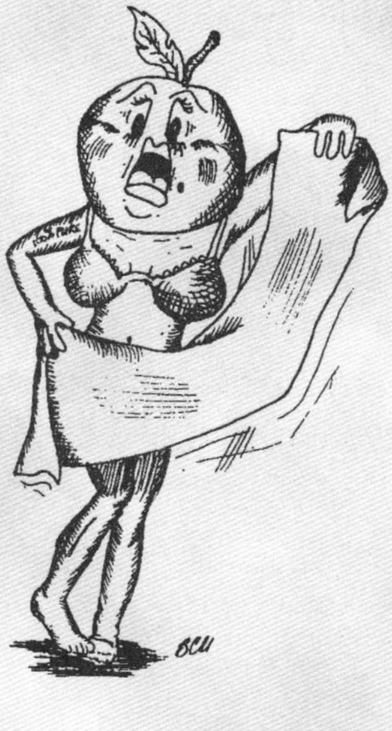

Spinach Salad

Lyn Arikado
Nakusp, BC

"You'll be strong to the finish when you eat this spinach!"
– Popeye

DRESSING:		
Sliced water chestnuts, drained	8 oz.	227 mL
Sugar	1 1/2 tbsp.	22 mL
Salt	1/2 tsp.	2 mL
Dry mustard	1/2 tsp.	2 mL
Cider vinegar	3 tbsp.	45 mL
Vegetable oil	1/4-1/3 cup	60-75 mL
Onion slice	1	1
Tarragon, pinch (optional)		
Large spinach bunch, torn in bite sized pieces	1	1
Bacon, cooked and crumbled	1/2 lb.	250 g
OPTIONAL:		
Cheddar cheese, shredded	1/2 cup	125 mL
Fresh mushrooms, sliced	3/4 cup	175 mL
Hard boiled eggs, chopped	2	2
Diced ham	1/2 cup	125 mL
Croutons	3/4 cup	175 mL

Mix together all dressing ingredients. Refrigerate 1 hour.

When ready to serve, put spinach into large serving bowl. Toss in bacon. Remove onion slice from dressing. Gently toss dressing into spinach. Add any optional ingredients and serve immediately. Serves 6.

Pictured on page 89.

Cottage Stuffed Tomatoes

Judy Hunter
Nelson, BC

Served as a side dish or for your luncheon. Serve in a bed of lettuce with a fresh bun or piece of herb toast.

Bacon slices	8	8
Mayonnaise	2 tbsp.	30 mL
Vinegar	2 tsp.	10 mL
Dried basil	1/4 tsp.	1 mL
Celery, diced	1/2 cup	125 mL
Cottage cheese	1 1/2 cups	375 mL
Fresh tomatoes, serving size	4	4
Salt, to taste		

In a skillet cook bacon until crisp. Drain, reserving 1 tbsp. (15 mL) bacon drippings. Crumble bacon and set aside.

In a bowl combine reserved bacon drippings, mayonnaise, vinegar, basil and crisp bacon.

In another bowl, stir together celery and cottage cheese. Add bacon mixture. Cover and let sit for one hour in refrigerator.

To serve: Cut stem ends from tomatoes. Place tomatoes cut sides down. Cut each tomato into sixths to within 1 inch (2.5 cm) of bottom. Carefully spread out sections, forming a "flower." Sprinkle with salt and fill each with equal amount of cheese mixture. Serves 4.

Pictured on page 35.

Elaine's Gem Salad

Elaine Gustafson
Burton, B.C.

"I call this Gem Salad because the small, bright vegetables look like jewels in the white surround."

Creamed cottage cheese	2 cups	500 mL
Tomato, finely cubed	1	1
Green pepper, finely cubed	1/3 cup	75 mL
Dill weed	1 tsp.	5 mL
Light mayonnaise	1/4 cup	60 mL
Ranch dressing	2 tbsp.	30 mL
Salt and pepper, to taste		

Mix all ingredients together in a bowl. Let marinate in refrigerator for 1/2 hour before serving. Serves 4-6.

Variation: Mix in peeled cucumber or avocado instead of green peppers.

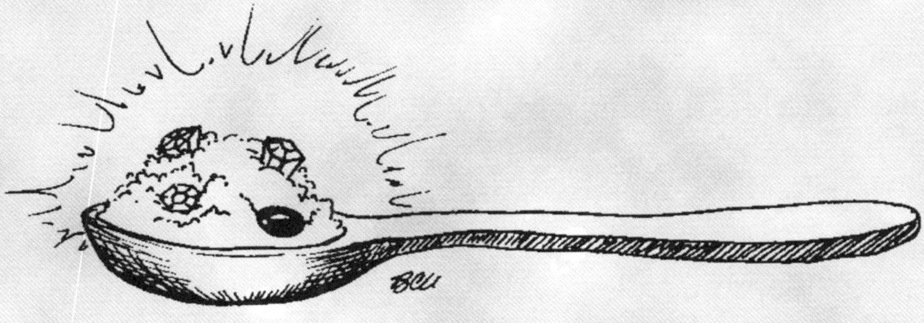

DID YOU KNOW: One half cup of creamed cottage cheese (120 calories) has about the same amount of protein as a 2-ounce serving of cooked meat, poultry or fish, or 2 slices cheddar cheese, or 2 eggs.

Sui Choy Salad

Pat and Jan Dion
Nakusp, BC

Sui choy is also known as Chinese cabbage. It has crinkly leaves and a weak cabbage flavor. You can find it among the Chinese greens in your supermarket.

Sui choy, large	1	1
Green onions, diced	5	5
Almonds, sliced	1/2 cup	125 mL
Sesame seeds	1/2 cup	125 mL
Butter OR margarine	1/4 cup	60 mL
Steam fried chinese noodles, crumbled	2 oz.	56 g
White vinegar	1/4 cup	60 mL
White sugar	1/2 cup	125 mL
Soya sauce	1 tsp.	5 mL
Peanut oil	1/2 cup	125 mL

Wash, remove large veins and chop sui choy into fine strips. Put in salad bowl. Toss in onions and set aside in refrigerator.

In small skillet, brown almonds and sesame seeds in butter. Remove from heat and mix in dry noodles.

Blend together remaining 4 ingredients in a bowl.

To serve: Combine almond mixture into sui choy. Toss with dressing. Serves 6.

Pictured on page 35.

DID YOU KNOW... There are 7 natural hotsprings in the Kootenay Country region where only 2 are commercial.

Sourgrass Salad

Elaine Gustafson
Burton, B.C.

"The Sourgrass adds a nice tang." Sourgrass is also known as sheep sorrel. This edible weed is rich in vitamin C.

Sourgrass, torn	1 cup	250 mL
Lettuce, torn	1 cup	250 mL
Tomato, thin wedges	1	1
Celery, chopped	1/2 cup	125 mL
Radishes, thin wedges	4-5	4-5
Onion, finely diced	1 tbsp.	15 mL

Toss ingredients together in salad bowl. Use your favorite dressing.

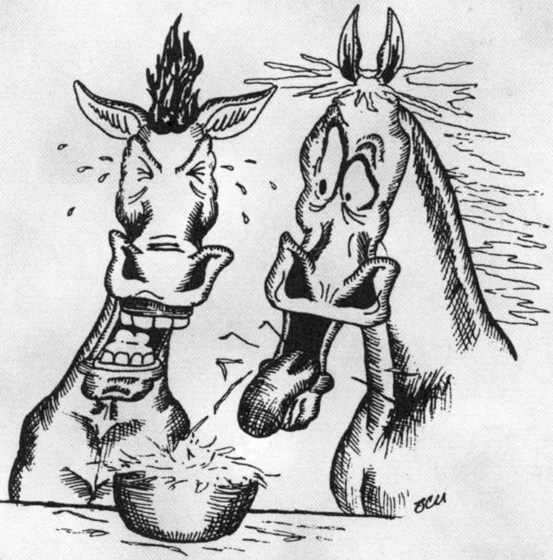

DID YOU KNOW... When hiking - if you are thirsty and have no water, chew 3 or 4 sour grass leaves as it relieves thirst.

Pesto Tortellini Salad

Hazel Calder
New Denver, BC

A favorite lunch salad. It is complimented with garlic toast on page 93.

Tortellini	7 oz.	196 g
Small red pepper, sliced	1	1
Carrot, sliced	1	1
Broccoli flowerets	3/4 cup	175 mL
Green or black olives, halved	1/3 cup	75 mL
DRESSING:		
Pesto	1/3 cup	75 mL
Milk	1/4 cup	60 mL
Mayonnaise	3/4 cup	175 mL
Grated Parmesan cheese	2 tbsp.	30 mL
Olive oil	1 tbsp.	15 mL
Pepper	1/2 tsp.	2 mL
Garlic clove, minced	1	1

Cook tortellini according to directions. Rinse in cold water. Transfer into salad bowl.

Gently toss red pepper, carrot, broccoli and olives into tortellini.

Combine dressing ingredients together. Mix well. Pour over salad and toss. Chill for 5 hours. Serves 4-6.

Variation: May be served in lettuce or spinach lined bowl.

Pictured on page 35.

Best Baked Beans

My sister Betty passed this recipe to my sister Marilyn, who then passed it on to me. Only the praised recipes get passed on.

Can pork and beans	19 oz.	540 mL
Chopped bacon, cooked	1/2 lb.	250 g
Brown sugar	1 tbsp.	15 mL
Molasses	1 tbsp.	15 mL
Dry mustard	1/2 tsp.	2 mL
Worcestershire sauce	1/2 tsp.	2 mL
Small onion, chopped	1	1
Butter OR margarine	1 tbsp.	15 mL

Mix together first 6 ingredients in 1-quart (1 L) casserole dish.

In a small skillet, sauté onion in butter. Mix with beans and bake in 350°F (175°C) oven for 1 hour. Serves 4.

Variation: Add cut up weiners for "weiners & beans".

Pictured on page 71.

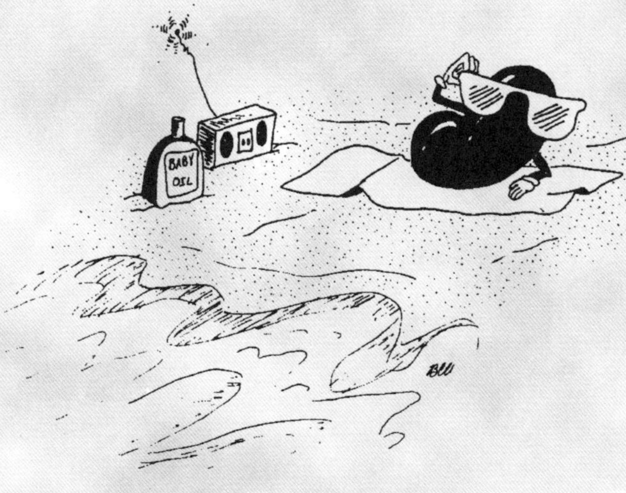

Corn with Mushrooms

Jenny Shkurhan
Wynndel, BC

Onion, chopped	2 tbsp.	30 mL
Fresh mushrooms, chopped	$^{2}/_{3}$ cup	150 mL
Butter OR margarine	2 tbsp.	30 mL
Niblets corn, drained	$1^{1}/_{2}$ cups	375 mL
Salt	$^{1}/_{8}$ tsp.	0.5 mL
Pepper, dash		
Whipping cream	$^{1}/_{4}$ cup	60 mL

In a skillet sauté onion and mushrooms in butter for 5 minutes on medium heat.

Stir in corn, salt and pepper with onions. Heat through. Stir in cream, heat and serve. Makes 4 servings.

Lemon Basil Carrots

Hazel Calder
New Denver, BC

Baby carrots	1 lb.	500 g
Butter OR margarine	2 tbsp.	30 mL
Lemon juice	1 tbsp.	15 mL
Garlic salt	$^{1}/_{2}$ tsp.	2 mL
Dried basil, crushed	$^{1}/_{2}$ tsp.	2 mL
Pepper, dash		

Steam carrots until tender.

In a small saucepan melt butter. Stir in remaining 4 ingredients. Add carrots and toss to mix. Serves 4-6.

Honey Mustard Carrots

Tammy Meisner
Beasley, BC

Serve in a white dish to bring out the vibrant orange, yellow and green colors. Tastes as good as it looks.

Large carrots, julienne sliced	6	6
Prepared mustard	1/4 cup	60 mL
Honey	1/2 cup	125 mL
Butter OR margarine	1/4 cup	60 mL
Chives OR parsley, chopped	2 tbsp.	30 mL
Salt and pepper, to taste		

In a medium saucepan, cook carrots in small amount of boiling water until crisp-tender.

Combine mustard, honey and butter in small saucepan. Cook on medium heat until well blended and heated through (can be heated in microwave). Drain carrots and place in serving dish. Pour mustard sauce on top and garnish with chives, salt and pepper. Makes 4 servings.

Pictured on page 53.

DID YOU KNOW... Based on 1995 Tourism BC Statistics, approximately 2.5 million tourists travel through the Kootenay Country each year.

Broccoli Casserole

Mom Smith impressed all of us when she served us this dish many years ago. A delightful broccoli and cheese dish.

Cream of mushroom soup	10 oz.	284 mL
Mayonnaise	1 cup	250 mL
Egg, slightly beaten	2	2
Small onion, grated	1	1
Frozen or fresh broccoli, chopped	2 1/2 cups	625 mL
Sharp cheddar cheese, shredded	1 cup	250 mL
Fine cracker or bread crumbs	1/2 cup	125 mL

In a 1 1/2-quart (1.5 L) casserole dish, combine soup, mayonnaise, eggs and onion. Stir in broccoli (if using frozen, thaw and drain) and cheese. Sprinkle top with cracker crumbs. Bake in 400°F (205°C) oven for 20 minutes or till lightly browned and bubbly. Serves 6.

Hash Browns To Order

Beth Guillaume
Warfield, BC

Favorite among family and friends.

Frozen hash browns	2 lbs.	1 kg
Sour cream	2 cups	500 mL
Cream of mushroom soup	2x 10 oz.	2x 284 mL
Butter OR margarine, melted	1/2 cup	125 mL
Cheddar cheese, grated	2 cups	500 mL
Grated onion, to taste		
Salt, to taste		
Grated parmesan cheese, to taste		

Hash Browns To Order
Continued...

Mix together first 7 ingredients in large bowl. Transfer into 9 x 13 inch (22 x 33 cm) baking dish. Sprinkle parmesan cheese on top. Bake in 350°F (175°C) oven for 1 to 1 1/2 hours Makes 6-8 servings. Freezes well.

Pan Fried Red Cabbage

Dreana Ratcliffe
Nakusp, BC

Adds a nice color to your dinner table.

Red cabbage, shredded	4 cups	500 mL
Brown sugar	2 tbsp.	30 mL
Garlic, crushed	1/2 tsp.	2 mL
Salt and pepper, to taste		
Oil	2 tbsp.	30 mL
Water	1 tbsp.	15 mL

In a large skillet, stir fry cabbage, brown sugar, garlic, salt and pepper in oil until heated through.

Stir in water, cover and cook over low heat until tender, about 5 minutes. Serves 4-6.

Pictured on page 53.

DID YOU KNOW... By lining the crisper section of your refrigerator with newspaper and wrapping vegetables with it, moisture will be absorbed and your vegetables will stay fresher longer.

Quick Chinese Stir Fry

Mary Orr
Nakusp, BC

A quick dinner when vegetables are prepared a head of time.

Oil	2 tbsp.	30 mL
Clove garlic, minced	1	1
Ginger root (minced)	2 tbsp.	30 mL
Broccoli, bite size pieces	2 cups	500 mL
Carrot, sliced julienne	1	1
Water	1/4 cup	60 mL
Green onion, chopped	1	1
Small onion, wedged	1	1
Mushrooms, halved	1/2 cup	125 mL
Small red pepper, chopped	1	1
Water	1/4 cup	60 mL
Cornstarch	1 tbsp.	15 mL
Sugar	1/2 tsp.	2 mL
Sesame oil, drops	2	2
Oyster sauce	1 tbsp.	15 mL

Heat wok on high heat. Add oil. Stir in garlic and ginger root. Add broccoli and stir for 3 minutes.

Stir in carrots with water, cover and cook 3 minutes.

Add onion, mushrooms and red pepper. Stir, cover and cook for another 5-7 minutes until tender.

In a bowl, combine water, cornstarch, sugar, sesame oil and oyster sauce. Make a well in vegetables and pour in cornstarch mixture. Stir until thickened. Serve on heated platter. Sprinkle with chopped green onions. Makes 2-4 servings.

Crispy Cheese Potatoes

Elizabeth Strong
Winlaw, BC

A cheesy potato with a crisp topping.

Medium potatoes, peeled and sliced	6	6
Butter OR margarine, melted	1/4 cup	60 mL
Seasoning salt, sprinkle		
Lemon pepper, to taste		
Cheddar cheese, grated	1 1/2 cups	375 mL
Cornflake crumbs	1 cup	250 mL

Layer potatoes in greased 9 x 9 inch (22 x 22 cm) baking pan. Pour butter over potatoes and sprinkle with seasoned salt and lemon pepper. Bake in 350°F (175°C) oven for 25 minutes.

Sprinkle cheese on potatoes and top with cornflakes. Bake for another 25-30 minutes until potatoes are tender. Serve with sour cream. Serves 6.

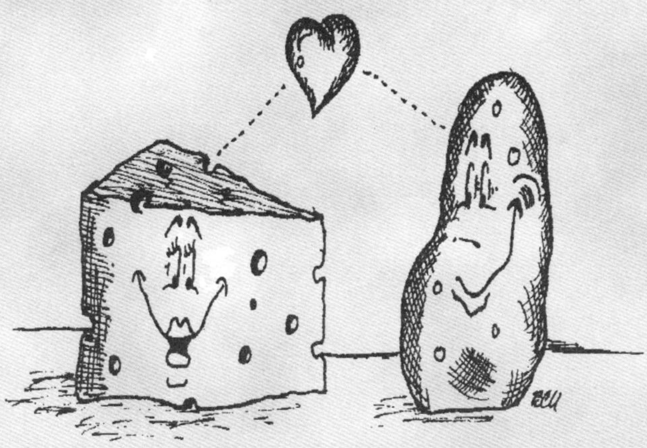

DID YOU KNOW... Cleaning screen tip. Rub a brush type hair roller lightly over the screen and see how easily it picks up all the lint and dust.

Zucchini Cutlets

Dreana Ratcliffe
Nakusp, BC

Another great way to impress your luncheon friends.

Medium zucchini, grated	3	3
Green onions, chopped	1/2 cup	125 mL
Carrots, grated	1/2 cup	125 mL
Green peppers, chopped	1/2 cup	125 mL
Garlic clove, chopped	1	1
Crackers, finely crushed	2 cups	500 mL
Flour	2 tbsp.	30 mL
Baking powder	1 tsp.	5 mL
Salt	3/4 tsp.	3 mL
Pepper	1/8 tsp.	0.5 mL
Eggs, beaten	2	2

In a bowl, combine first 10 ingredients. Mix well.

Stir in eggs. Form into patties. Fry in nonstick pan over medium heat for 10 minutes on each side, till lightly browned. Makes 8-10 cutlets.

Pictured on page 53.

Roasted Mustard Potatoes, page 55
Pan Fried Red Cabbage, page 49
Honey Mustard Carrots, page 47
Zucchini Cutlets, page 52

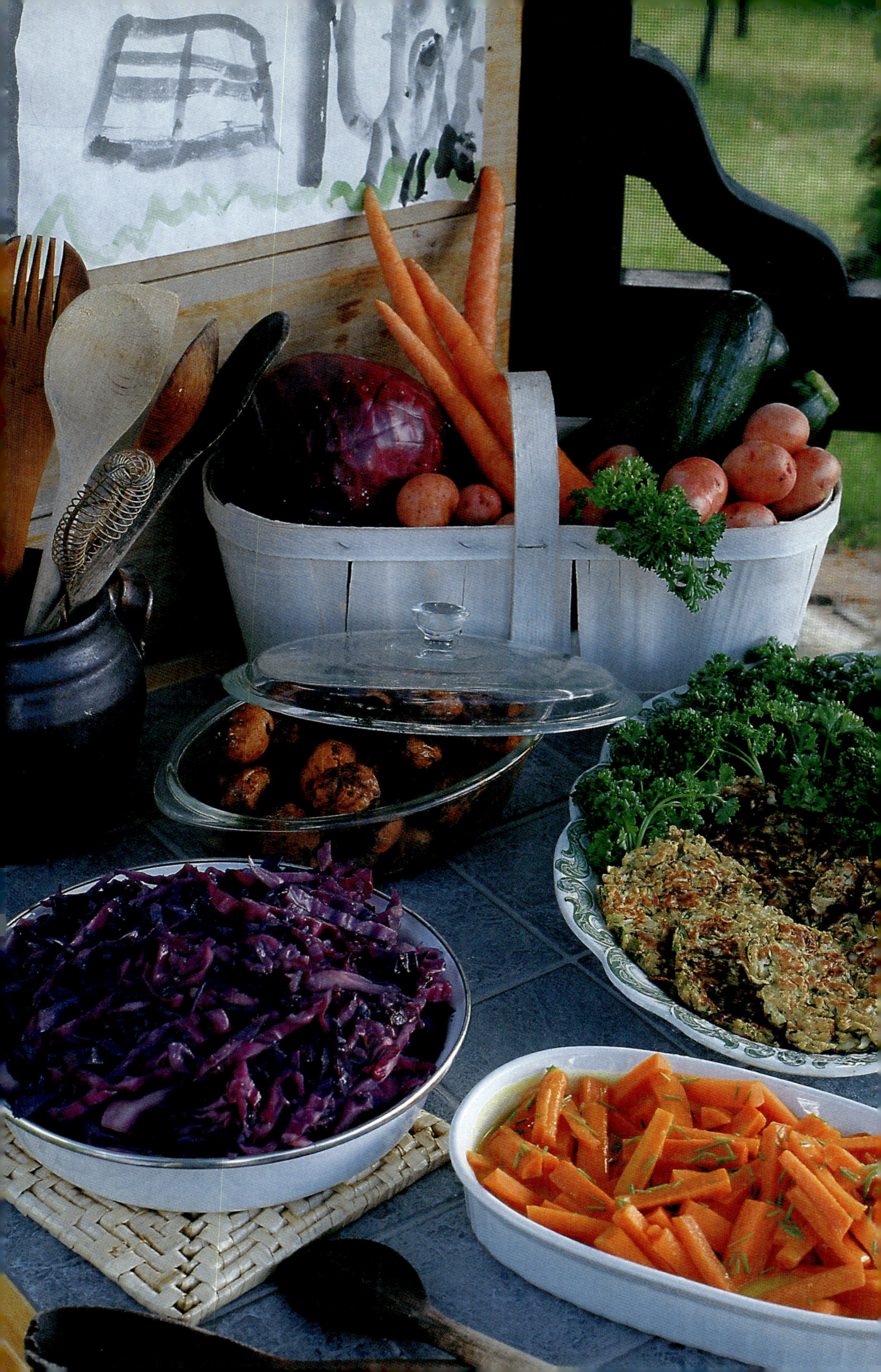

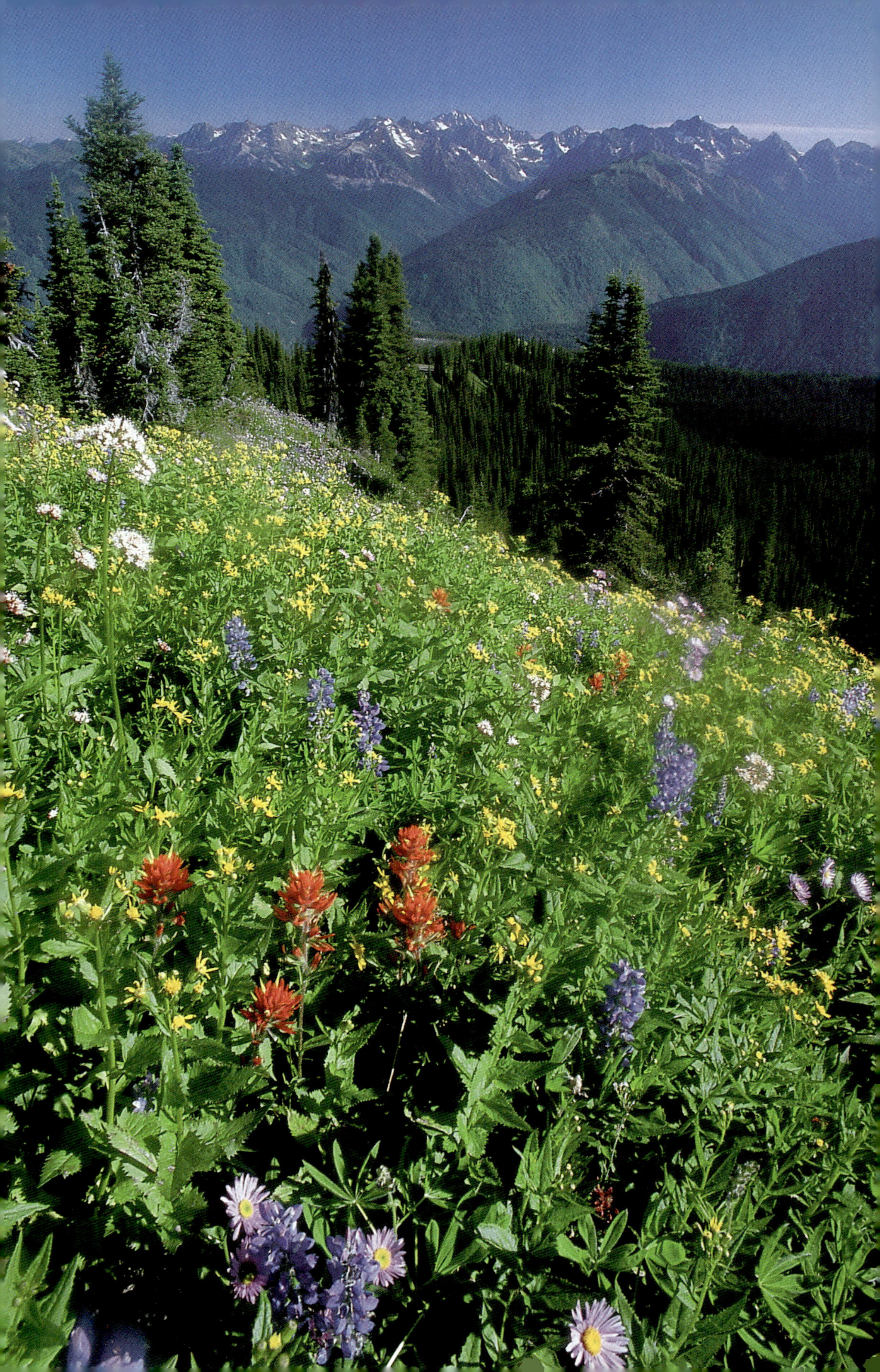

Roasted Mustard Potatoes

Sylvia Bowins
Creston, BC

"Each serving has only 137 calories and 1.7 g of fat."

Dijon style mustard	4 tbsp.	60 mL
Paprika	2 tsp.	10 mL
Ground cumin	1 tsp.	5 mL
Chili powder	1 tsp.	5 mL
Cayenne pepper	1/8 tsp.	0.5 mL
Red potatoes, very small	12	12

In a large bowl combine mustard, paprika, cumin, chili powder and cayenne pepper.

Prick potatoes several times with fork. Add to seasonings and toss to evenly coat potatoes. Put in greased baking pan. Bake in 400°F (205°C) oven for 45-60 minutes until potatoes are tender. Makes 4 servings.

Pictured on page 53.

DID YOU KNOW... In the Kootenay Country, there are approximately 841 Kilometers of hiking trails.

Wildflowers grace the sub alpine in Selkirk Mountains near the historic town of Sandon.

Green Beans Supreme

Lorraine Fadden
Creston, BC

"This is an excellent alternative to ordinary bean dishes."

Green OR lima beans, frozen	9 oz.	252 g
Small onion, sliced	1	1
Parsley flakes	1 tsp.	5 mL
Butter OR margarine	3 tbsp.	45 mL
White flour	2 tbsp.	30 mL
Lemon peel, grated	1/2 tsp.	2 mL
Salt and pepper, to taste		
Milk	1/2 cup	125 mL
Sour cream	1 cup	250 mL
Cheddar cheese, grated	1/2 cup	125 mL
Dry bread crumbs	1/4 cup	60 mL

In a saucepan, cook beans until tender. Drain.

In a separate saucepan, sauté onion and parsley in 2 tbsp. (30 mL) butter until onion is transparent. Stir in flour, lemon peel, salt and pepper. Add milk and stir until thickened. Mix in sour cream and the cooked beans. Heat until bubbly. Spoon into 1-quart (1 L) casserole dish and sprinkle with cheese.

Melt remaining butter and toss with bread crumbs. Sprinkle over bean mixture. Broil for 2-3 minutes until cheese melts. Serves 4.

DID YOU KNOW... The Creston Valley Wildlife Centre indicates that you may find approximately 100 Tundra Swans at the south end of Kootenay Lake and the north end of Duck Lake in February/ March and October/November.

Garlic Ribs

Terri Hanson
Nakusp, B.C.

Moist, tender and delicious.

Beef OR pork ribs, cut in bite sized pieces	4 lbs.	2 kg
Water	8 cups	2 L
Sugar	1/2 cup	125 mL
Brown sugar	1/2 cup	125 mL
Molasses	2 tbsp.	30 mL
Soya sauce	1/2 cup	125 mL
Black tea	1 cup	250 mL
Garlic cloves, crushed	3-5	3-5

Place ribs in large pot and cover with water. Bring to a boil. Reduce heat, cover and simmer 40 minutes. Drain.

In a bowl, mix together next 6 ingredients. Put ribs into sauce and simmer for 30-45 minutes. Serve with rice. Enjoy!

Variation: Chicken wings or breasts can be substituted for the ribs. Can be baked instead of boiled.

Pictured on page 71.

DID YOU KNOW... Laundry tip: For the whitest socks, boil in water to which a lemon slice has been added.

Aaron's Pizazzie Pizza

The Fred Walker School - Food and Nutrition Program
Grand Forks, BC

Guaranteed to be a favorite pizza pie - students in the Fred Walker School Food and Nutrition program ate every last piece and talked about it for days!

CRUST:

Granulated sugar	1 tbsp.	15 mL
Active dry yeast	1 tbsp.	15 mL
Warm water	1/4 cup	60 mL
Olive oil	2 tbsp.	30 mL
Salt	1 tsp.	5 mL
Warm water	1 cup	250 mL
Whole wheat flour, OR unbleached white	3 3/4 cups	875 mL
Butter OR margarine, melted	1/4 cup	60 mL
Garlic cloves, crushed	3-5	3-5

TOPPINGS: Tomato paste, sliced hot peppers, diced green peppers, diced onions, crushed pineapple, thinly sliced ham, Cheddar and Mozzarella cheese.

In a bowl, dissolve sugar and yeast in water. Let sit 10 minutes.

In a large bowl, combine oil, salt and water. Stir in yeast mixture. Beat in half flour. Stir in more flour until dough is smooth. Turn onto floured surface and knead in remaining flour. Knead for 8 minutes. Divide dough in half and press into two 10 inch (25 cm) lightly oiled pans. Cover and let rise in room temperature for 15 minutes.

"Now for the real pizazz. Melt some butter with lots and lots of garlic. With a pastry brush, spread liberal amounts of garlic butter onto your crust." Add toppings. Bake in 450°F (230°C) oven for 20 minutes or until done. Makes 2 large pizzas.

Steak Nancy

Nancy Savage
Trout Lake, BC

A winner on any menu!

Butter OR margarine	1 cup	250 mL
Small garlic clove, crushed	1	1
Salt	3/4 tsp.	3 mL
Pepper	1/2 tsp.	2 mL
Round steak	2 lbs.	1 kg
Lemon, quartered	1	1
Worcestershire sauce	1/2 tsp.	2 mL
Onion, chopped	3/4 tsp.	3 mL

In a bowl, cream together butter, garlic, salt and pepper until smooth. Chill.

Cut steak into 6-8 oz. (170 g-250 g) serving pieces. Pound each piece to 1/4 inch (0.5 cm) thickness.

In a large skillet, heat half butter mixture until hot. Add steak pieces and brown each side. Remove and keep warm.

Rub sides of skillet with lemon quarters. Squeeze juice into drippings. Add remaining butter mixture, worcestershire sauce and onion Reduce heat until butter browns. Add meat and simmer 5 minutes, basting with drippings. Serve with mashed potatoes using drippings as gravy. Enjoy! Makes 4-6 servings.

DID YOU KNOW... Trout Lake has 2 working heritage, original Kootenay, hand-operated gravity fed gas pumps which are dated 1904 and 1915.

Oriental Hamburger Casserole

Lucille Wells
Nakusp, BC

"Great served with stir fried vegetables."

Ground beef	1 1/2 lbs.	750 g
Large onion, chopped	1	1
Celery, chopped	1 1/2 cups	375 mL
Soya sauce	2 tbsp.	30 mL
Rice, uncooked	1/2 cup	125 mL
Water	1 1/2 cup	375 mL
Sliced mushrooms, drained	10 oz.	284 mL
Cream of chicken soup	10 oz.	284 mL
Pepper,to taste		
Chow mein noodles	1 cup	250 mL

In a large skillet, brown ground beef. Drain.

Mix onion and celery into ground beef. Cook for 2 minutes and add remaining 6 ingredients. Cover and simmer for 1 1/2 hours, stirring occasionally. Transfer to casserole dish. Top with chow mein noodles and bake in a 350°F (175°C) oven for 15 minutes. Serves 6.

Variation: Mix all ingredients in 3-quart (3 L) casserole dish. Cover and bake in 325°F (160°C) oven for 1 hour. Top with noodles and bake uncovered for another 30 minutes.

Hobo Stew Casserole

Betsy-Ann Gallinger
Crawford Bay, BC

A hearty warming dish on a cool night.

Large potatoes, sliced	4	4
Kidney beans	14 oz.	398 mL
Onion, chopped	1	1
Celery, chopped	1/2 cup	125 mL
Salt	1 tsp.	5 mL
Pepper, to taste		
Ground beef	1 lb.	500 g
Tomato soup	10 oz.	284 mL

Layer potatoes in greased 2-quart (2 L) casserole dish. Layer with kidney beans, onion, celery, salt and pepper. Top with ground beef and tomato soup. Cover and bake in 350°F (175°C) oven for 1 1/2-2 hours, till done. Serves 4-6.

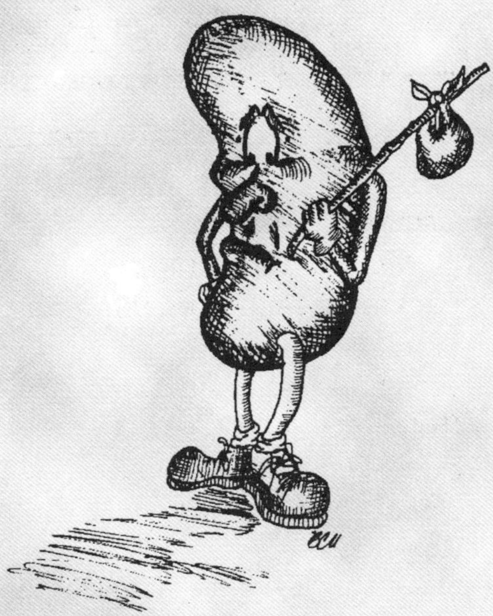

Simple Delicious Meatballs

Jann Shubin
Crawford Bay, BC

A quick meatball dish with a nice taste.

Ground beef	1 lb.	500 g
Brown sugar	1 cup	250 mL
Vinegar	3/4 cup	175 mL
Cold Water	3/4 cup	175 mL
Ketchup	3/4 cup	175 mL
Dry mustard	1 tbsp.	15 mL

Form ground beef into about 20 meatballs and brown in skillet. Transfer to 1 1/2-quart (1.5 L) casserole dish.

In a bowl, mix together remaining 5 ingredients. Pour over meatballs. Bake uncovered in 350°F (175°C) oven for 1 hour. Serve with rice or pasta. Serves 4.

World's Best Burritos

According to my niece Jennifer, these are "the best".

Ground beef	1 lb.	500 g
Medium onion, chopped	2/3 cup	150 mL
Packaged taco seasoning mix	1/2	1/2
Pepper	1/8 tsp.	0.5 mL
Oregano	1/8 tsp.	0.5 mL
Parsley	1/8 tsp.	0.5 mL
Sour cream	1/2 cup	125 mL
Cheddar cheese, grated	4 cups	1 L
Taco sauce	1/3 cup	75 mL
Flour tortillas	10	10

World's Best Burritos
Continued...

In a skillet, brown ground beef and onion. Drain. Add taco seasoning, pepper, oregano, parsley and sour cream. Mix well. Stir in half cheese and half taco sauce.

Roll 2-3 tbsp. (30-45 mL) of mixture in flour tortillas. Place in greased casserole dish. Top with remaining cheese and taco sauce. Bake uncovered in 350°F (175°C) oven for 15 minutes or until cheese melts and burritos are heated through. Makes 10.

Sweet & Sour Garlic Ribs

Kathy Mackenzie
Nakusp, BC

"This recipe was passed on to me by my mom. It's a zesty recipe and a family favorite."

Ribs, cut in bite sized pieces	4 lbs.	2 kg
Barbecue sauce	1 cup	250 mL
Ketchup	1 cup	250 mL
Water	1 cup	250 mL
Sugar	1/2 cup	125 mL
Onion, chopped	1 cup	250 mL
Garlic cloves, minced	3	3
Worcestershire sauce	1 tsp.	5 mL
Bay leaves	2	2

Put ribs in baking pan. Set aside

In a medium saucepan, combine remaining 8 ingredients. Boil for 15 minutes. Pour over ribs. Bake in 350°F (175°C) oven for 2 hours until meat is tender. Remove bay leaves. Serve with rice.

Variation: Use chicken pieces instead of ribs.

Sweet & Sour Meatballs

Marilyn & Eric Guillaume's Kitchen

These meatballs originated in Manitoba. They are a very popular catering dish for Ukrainian weddings.

Ground beef	1 1/2 lbs.	750 g
Bread crumbs	1/2 cup	125 mL
Onion, minced	1/2 cup	125 mL
Egg, beaten	1	1
Water	1/2 cup	125 mL
Salt	1 1/2 tsp.	7 mL
Pepper	1/4 tsp.	1 mL
Water	1 cup	250 mL
Ketchup	1 cup	250 mL
Salt	1 tsp.	5 mL
Cayenne pepper, dash		
Worcestershire sauce	2 tbsp.	30 mL
Sugar	1/2 cup	125 mL
Vinegar	3 tbsp.	45 mL

Put first 7 ingredients in bowl. Mix together well. Shape into small balls. Place on baking pan and bake in 350°F (175°C) oven for 10 minutes. Turn balls and bake another 10-15 minutes. Transfer balls into a 2-quart (2.5 L) casserole dish.

Combine remaining 7 ingredients in a saucepan. Bring to a boil. Pour over meatballs and bake in 325°F (160°C) oven for 1 hour. Makes 46 meatballs.

Pictured on page 71.

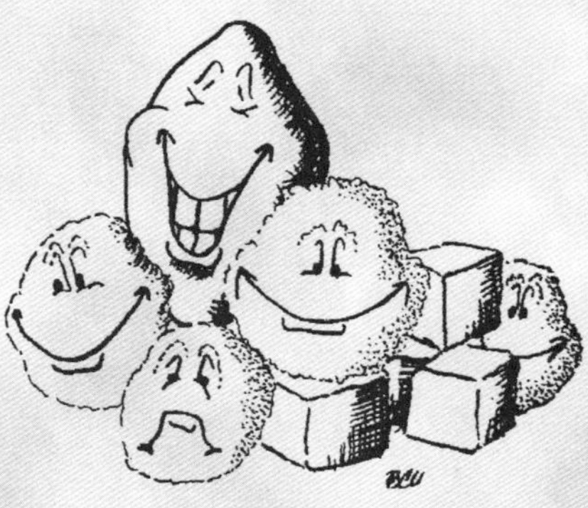

Aju De Gallina – Peruvian Chicken

Pat and Jan Dion
Nakusp, BC

"Serve this dish with rice and yams for a traditional meal."

Chicken pieces	2-3 lbs.	1-1.5 kg
Cooking oil	1/4 cup	60 mL
Large onion, diced	1	1
Garlic cloves, minced	3	3
Tomatoes, diced	2	2
Salt	1 tsp.	5 mL
White bread slices, small cubes	10	10
Jalapeño peppers, chopped	2	2
Evaporated milk	2x 13.5 oz	2x 385 mL
Chicken broth	2 cups	500 mL
Grated parmesan cheese	1 cup	250 mL

In a large skillet, lightly brown chicken in oil, about 15 minutes. Transfer chicken to 9 x 13 inch (22 x 33 cm) baking pan.

Fry onion and garlic in same skillet. Add to baking pan with tomatoes. Sprinkle with salt.

Blend bread and peppers in bowl or food processor. Mix in evaporated milk and broth. Pour over chicken and cover with parmesan cheese. Bake in a 350°F (175°C) oven for 1 hour. Serves 6 generous portions.

Variation: Prepare in slow cooker other than baking pan. Slow cook on low for 6-8 hours.

Cinnamon Chicken

Jenny Shkurhan
Wynndel, B.C

"This spice mixture may sound strange, but the flavor is delicious! Great for picnics as it is good cold as well as hot."

COATING		
Flour	$1\frac{1}{2}$ cups	375 mL
Salt	2 tsp.	10 mL
Celery salt	1 tsp.	5 mL
Pepper	2 tsp.	10 mL
Allspice	1 tsp.	5 mL
Ground cinnamon	$\frac{1}{2}$ tsp.	2 mL
Chicken pieces	3 lbs.	1.5 kg
Milk OR light cream	$\frac{1}{2}$ cup	125 mL
Butter OR margarine	1 tbsp.	15 mL
Cooking oil	2 tbsp.	30 mL

Measure first 6 ingredients into bowl. Stir.

Dip chicken in milk and coat with flour coating.

Heat butter and oil in skillet. Add coated chicken and brown 10-15 minutes each side. Lower heat and cook until tender, about 20 minutes. Turn often. Serves 4 to 6.

Pictured on page 71.

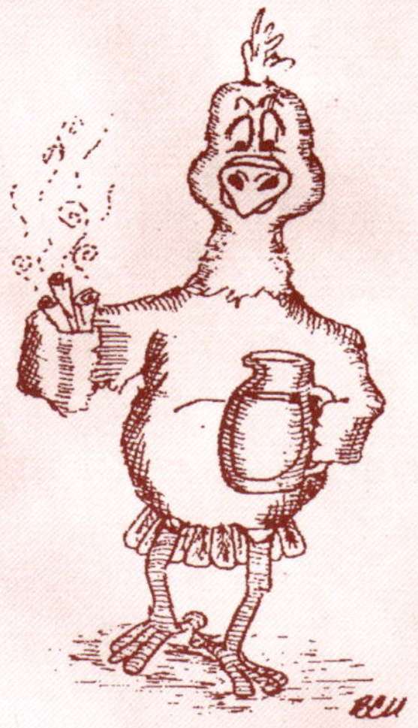

Soo-Kai Almond Chicken

Kelley Buckley
Nakusp, BC

Boneless chicken breasts, skinned	2	2
Soya sauce	1 tsp.	5 mL
Sugar	1 tsp.	5 mL
Wine	1/4 cup	60 mL
Corn starch	2 tsp.	10 mL
Salt, pinch		
Bread crumbs, fine	1 1/2 cups	375 mL
Ground almonds	3 tbsp.	45 mL
Flour	1/4 cup	60 mL
Eggs	2	2
Water	2 tbsp.	30 mL
GRAVY:		
Chicken stock	1 cup	250 mL
sugar	1/2 tsp.	2 mL
Soya sauce	1/2 tsp.	2 mL
Cornstarch	3 tsp.	15 mL

Marinate chicken breasts in the soya sauce, sugar, wine, cornstarch and salt for approximately 10 minutes.

In a bowl, mix together bread crumbs, almonds and flour. Set aside.

In another bowl, beat eggs with water. Dip chicken in eggs and coat with bread crumb mixture. Fry in 2 tbsp. (30 mL) oil on both sides till brown.

In a saucepan, combine all gravy ingredients and cook on low heat until thickened. To serve, cut chicken into strips and place on bed of sliced lettuce. Pour gravy over top. Sprinkle chopped almonds on top.

Chicken Imperial

Auntie Dorothy

Wine brings out the finest taste and aroma. When wine is heated, the alcoholic content disappears, leaving only its subtle flavor.

Chicken breasts, halved	4	4
Flour	5 tbsp.	75 mL
Butter OR margarine	2 tbsp.	30 mL
Olive oil	2 tbsp.	30 mL
Fresh mushrooms, sliced	1 1/2 cups	375 mL
Onion, chopped	1 tbsp.	15 mL
Whipping cream	2/3 cup	150 mL
White wine	2/3 cup	150 mL
Salt	1/2 tsp.	2 mL
Pepper, pinch		

Coat chicken breasts with flour. Reserve flour.

In a skillet, melt butter with oil. Add chicken and cook on both sides until lightly browned. Remove chicken and set aside.

Add mushrooms and onion to skillet. Cook until onions are transparent. Stir in whipping cream, wine, salt and pepper. Add chicken, cover and simmer for 20 minutes or till chicken is tender. Remove chicken, keep warm.

Blend reserved flour with little water. Gradually stir in skillet till sauce is thickened. Spoon sauce over the chicken. Serve with pasta or rice. Serves 6-8.

DID YOU KNOW... To rid your cutting board of onion, garlic or fish smell, cut a lime or lemon in two and rub the surface with the cut side of the fruit.

Gordon's Bedeviled Chicken Curry

Gordon Brown
Kaslo, B.C.

"This is wonderful served over a rice dish and accompanied with Gingered Cucumber on page 34, fruit chutney and cashews."

Medium onions, chopped	4	4
Fresh ginger, minced or sliced	1 tbsp.	15 mL
Garlic, minced or sliced	1 tbsp.	15 mL
Olive oil	2 tbsp.	30 mL
Sesame oil	1 tbsp.	15 mL
Coconut milk	14 oz.	398 mL
Piece of soaked kafir lime skin, minced (optional)	1	1
Asian curry powder	2-4 tbsp.	30-60 mL
Ripe banana, sliced	1	1
Whole chicken, cut up	1	1
Fresh mushrooms, quartered	8	8

In a large skillet sauté onions, ginger and garlic in olive and sesame oils until onions are tender. Add coconut milk, kafir lime skin, curry powder and banana. Bring to boil, reduce heat and simmer 10 minutes.

Skin chicken pieces and remove fat. Put leg, thigh and wing pieces (reserving chicken breasts) into sauce. Bring to boil. Reduce heat, cover and simmer one hour.

Cube breast meat. Stir in breast cubes and mushrooms into skillet. Simmer another 30 minutes until tender. Serves 6.

Variation: Kafir lime skin (imported Asian dry lime skin), may be substituted with 2 tsp. (10 mL) lime zest.

Japanese Chicken

Marilyn & Eric Guillaume's Kitchen

The glaze makes this a favorite at large family gatherings.

Chicken drumettes	3 lbs.	1.5 kg
Egg, beaten	1	1
Flour	1 cup	250 mL
Soya sauce	3 tbsp.	45 mL
Water	3 tbsp.	45 mL
Sugar	1 cup	250 mL
Vinegar	1/2 cup	125 mL
Garlic cloves, crushed	3	3

Dip chicken drumettes in egg and coat in flour. Fry in 2 tbsp. (30 mL) oil until golden brown. Transfer to flat baking dish.

In a bowl combine remaining 5 ingredients. Pour over chicken. Bake in 350°F (175°C) oven for 1 hour. Baste frequently. Serve with rice. Makes 6 servings.

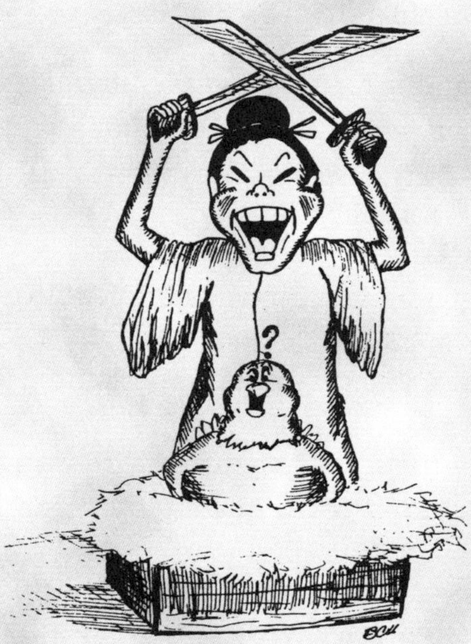

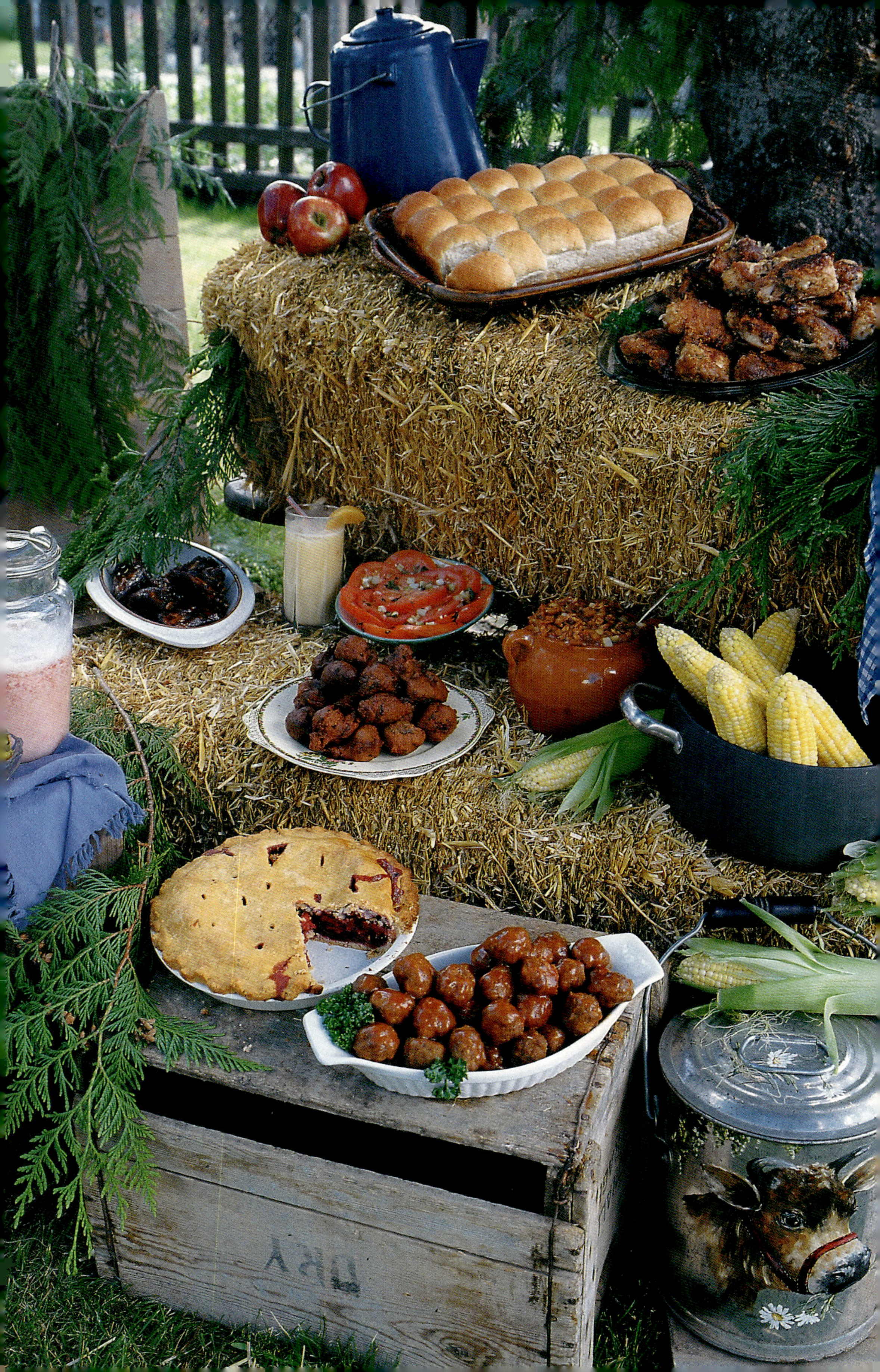

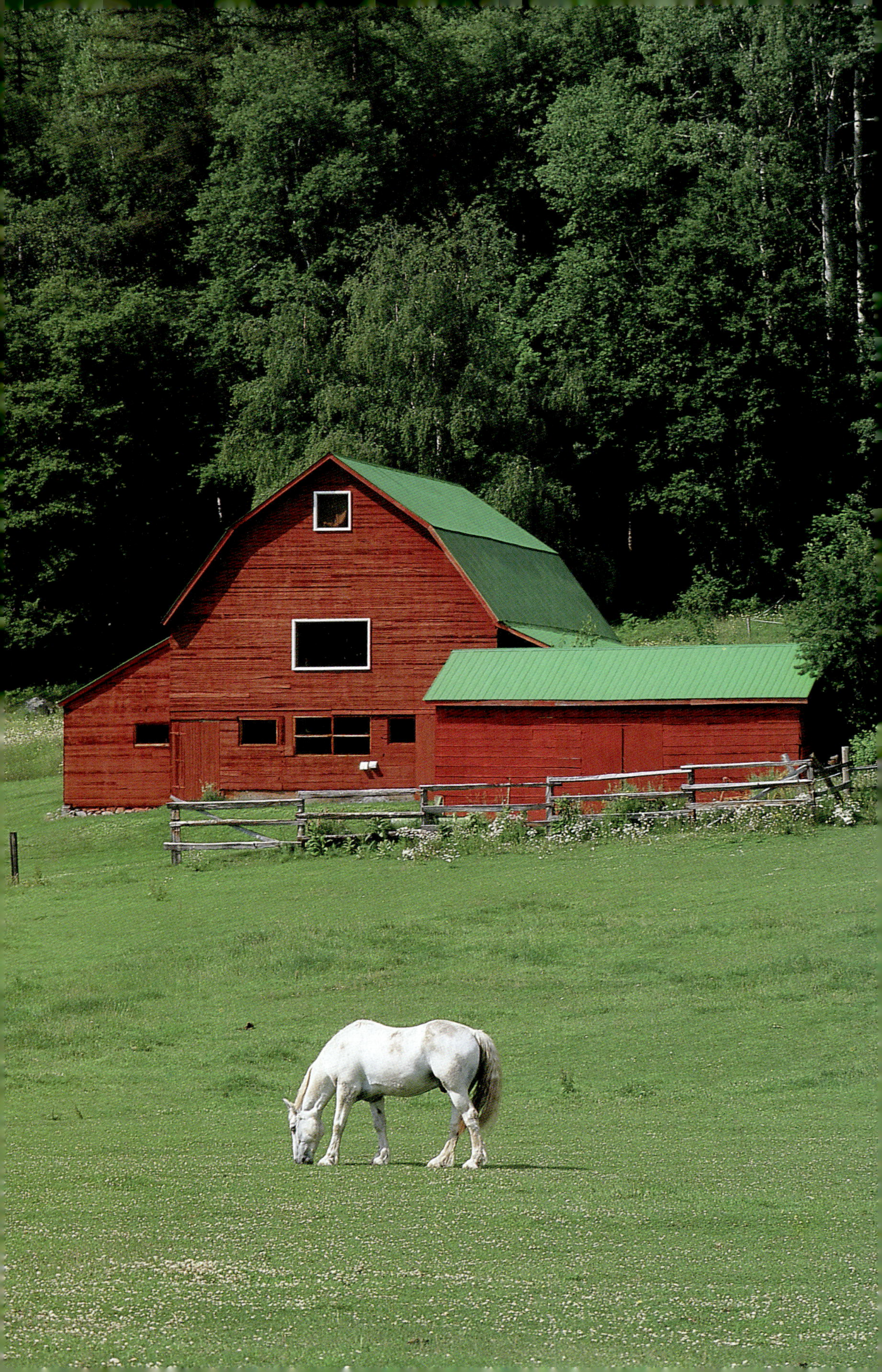

Honey Chicken Wings

A wonderful poultry dish using fresh local honey.

Chicken wings, disjointed	2 lbs.	1 kg
Pepper, to taste		
Honey	1 cup	250 mL
Soy sauce	1/2 cup	125 mL
Oil	2 tbsp.	30 mL
Ketchup	2 tbsp.	30 mL
Garlic clove, crushed	1	1

Season chicken with the pepper and place in a baking dish.

In a bowl, blend together honey, soy sauce, oil, ketchup and garlic. Pour over chicken. Bake in a 350°F (175°C) oven for 45 minutes. Serve with rice. Serves 4.

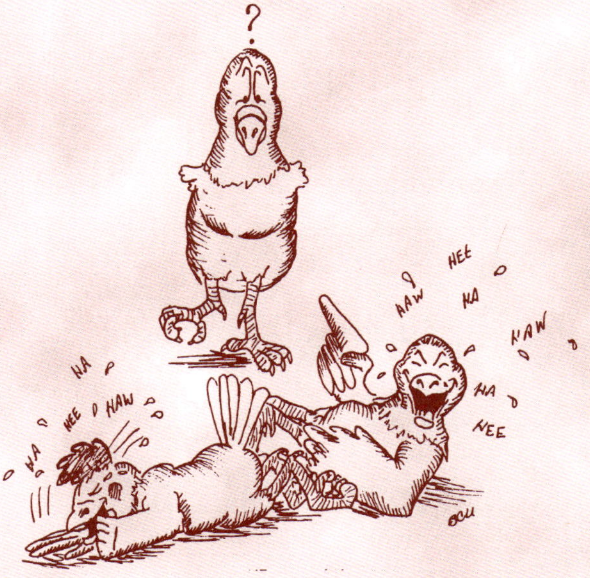

Tranquil country setting near New Denver in the Slocan Valley.

Barbecue Pizza

Barb Williams' and Cris Dawson's Kitchen
Nelson, BC

"Ever wish that you could get that wood burning stove pizza taste at home? Here is the way to get it! The prep work can be done in advance - then let your guests have fun making and BBQ'ing their own pizza!"

PIZZA CRUST:		
Flour	3 1/2 cups	825 mL
Instant yeast	1 tbsp.	15 mL
Sugar	1 tbsp.	15 mL
Salt	1 tsp.	5 mL
Optional, to taste: crushed garlic, rosemary, oregano, grated parmesan		
Hot water	1 1/2 cups	375 mL
Olive oil	2 tbsp.	30 mL
GRILLED TOMATO SAUCE:		
Large roma tomatoes, halved	8	8
Large onion, halved	1	1
Vegetable oil	2 tbsp.	30 mL
Garlic clove, crushed	1	1
Rosemary, chopped	1 tbsp.	15 mL
Balsamic vinegar	1 tbsp.	15 mL
Olive oil	2 tbsp.	30 mL
Black pepper, to taste		
GRILLED CHICKEN:		
Lemon juice	1/4 cup	60 mL
Olive oil	3 tbsp.	45 mL
Garlic cloves, crushed	4	4
Red pepper flakes	1/4 tsp.	1 mL
Black pepper, to taste		
Chicken breasts, boneless	2	2

Barbecue Pizza Continued...

OTHER TOPPING OPTIONS:
Sliced eggplant, small broccoli spears, whole or halved mushrooms, halved peppers (slice after grilling), pesto, olive oil

CHEESE TOPPING OPTIONS:
Feta, Mozzarella, Romano, Parmesan

Pizza crust: Combine dry ingredients together in large bowl. Add water and oil. Stir thoroughly to moisten. Turn out on lightly floured surface. Knead until smooth. Place dough in greased bowl, cover with plastic wrap and put in warm place to rise till double in size, about 1 hour. Punch down and refrigerate until ready to shape.

Grilled tomato sauce: Brush tomatoes and onion with oil and grill on barbecue (low heat) till soft and slightly charred. Cool and put in food processor or bowl. Add remaining five ingredients and blend until chunky. Refrigerate until ready to use.

Grilled chicken: Combine first five ingredients together. Add chicken and marinate in fridge for 2-6 hours. Grill on hot barbecue till tender. Cool slightly and cut into small pieces. Refrigerate until ready to use.

Other topping options: Brush vegetables with olive oil and grill on low heat until soft and lightly charred.

Putting it all together: The key to barbecuing pizza is indirect heat. You can accomplish this by placing an old cookie sheet right on top of the charcoal rocks. Barbecue on low heat. Shape 6" pizza crusts and place directly on grill. Close lid. Bake 5 to 10 minutes until top side of crust is bubbly. Remove crust from barbecue and coat raw side of crust in cornmeal (so it doesn't stick to grill). Place cornmeal coated side directly on grill and add favorite suggested toppings. ENJOY!

Chicken Rice Casserole

Jan Shubin
Crawford Bay, BC

Tasty and quick to prepare. You may add chopped green pepper, broccoli or carrots to this dish.

Hot water	3 cups	750 mL
Long grain rice, uncooked	2 cups	500 mL
Oil	1/3 cup	75 mL
Soya sauce	1/3 cup	75 mL
Packaged onion soup mix	1	1
Sliced mushrooms, undrained	10 oz.	284 mL
Chicken pieces	4-6	4-6

Mix together first 6 ingredients into 1 1/2-quart (1.5 L) casserole dish. Add chicken pieces. Cover and bake in 350°F (175°C) oven for 50-60 minutes or till chicken and rice are tender. Serves 4.

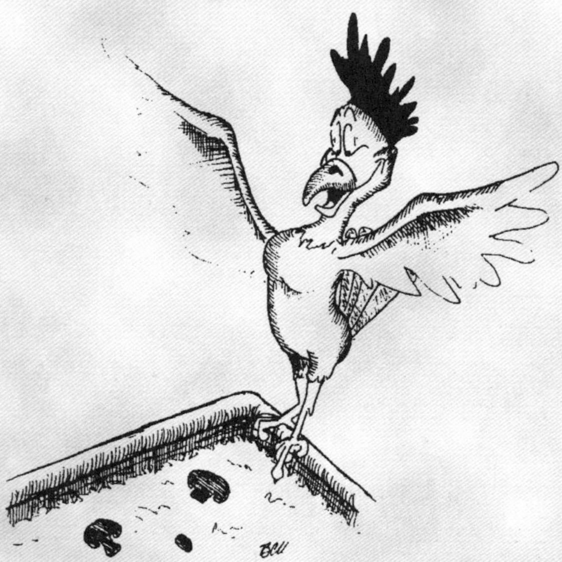

Hunters One-Dish Meal

Hazel Calder
New Denver, BC

Hunting season in the Kootenays is a happy time for hunters. This dish adds to the happiness.

Venison, cubed	1 1/2 lbs.	750 g
Onion, finely chopped	1	1
Celery, diced	1 cup	250 mL
Cooking oil	3 tbsp.	45 mL
Rice, uncooked	1/2 cup	125 mL
Water	1 cup	250 mL
Soya sauce	4 tsp.	20 mL
Cream of mushroom soup	10 oz.	284 mL
Cream of chicken soup	10 oz.	284 mL
Mushroom pieces, drained	10 oz.	284 mL
Peas	1 cup	250 mL
Salt, to taste		
Pepper, to taste		

Brown meat, onion and celery in the oil in skillet. Transfer to casserole dish.

In a bowl, mix together remaining 9 ingredients. Pour over meat and bake in 350°F (175°C) oven for 20-30 minutes, till rice is cooked. Serve with baking powder biscuits. Serves 4 hungry hunters.

DID YOU KNOW... The largest nontypical Elk in the world was taken in Shelter Bay in 1994. It scored 456 4/8.

Grouse and Wild Rice with Orange Sauce

Dreana Ratcliffe
Nakusp, BC

This quick and easy dish looks like a gourmet dinner.

Grouse breasts	4-6	4-6
Cooking oil	2 tbsp.	30 mL
ORANGE SAUCE:		
Orange juice	1 cup	250 mL
Butter OR margarine	1 tbsp.	15 mL
Flour	1 1/2 tbsp.	22 mL
Cooked wild rice	4 cups	1 L

In a skillet, fry grouse breasts in oil until tender.

Meanwhile, in a saucepan, mix together orange juice, butter and flour. Stir over medium heat until sauce thickens.

Serve grouse on a bed of wild rice. Pour orange sauce over top. Serve with favorite vegetables.

Pictured on cover.

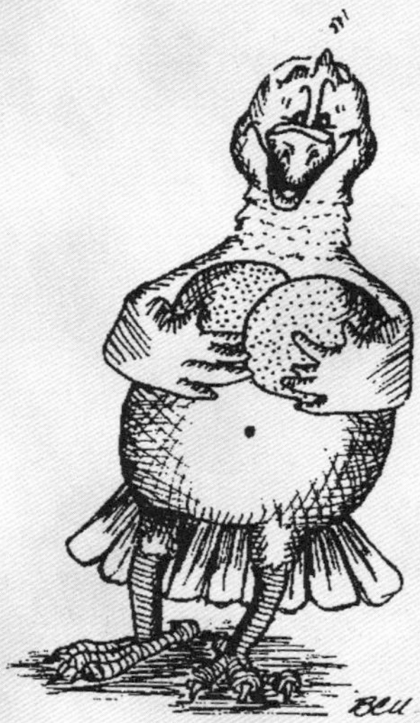

Trout Lake Lemon and Dill Cream Sauce

Allen Sorensen
Windsor Hotel
Trout Lake, BC

"This is an excellent sauce that goes superbly overtop any monster sized freshwater Kootenay fish."

Small onion, diced	1/4 cup	60 mL
Garlic, chopped	1 tsp.	5 mL
Butter or margarine	2 tbsp.	30 mL
Virgin olive oil	1 tbsp.	15 mL
Flour	1/3 cup	75 mL
Milk	2 cups	500 mL
Dill	2 tbsp.	500 mL
Worcestershire sauce	1/2 tsp.	2 mL
Lemon juice	1/3 cup	75 mL
Whipping cream	1/4 cup	60 mL
Salt, pinch		
Pepper, pinch		
Nutmeg, pinch		

In a skillet, sauté the first 4 ingredients together.

Stir in flour until well combined. Slowly stir in milk, bringing to a boil. Stir until desired thickness.

Strain sauce to remove the diced onions. Return to skillet and add remaining seven ingredients. Simmer for 20 minutes, stirring occasionally.

Pour over large prepared fish. Season to taste. Garnish with finely diced chives or green onions.

Caribou Rack Cutlets with Port & Stilton Sauce

Geoff Hampson
Mountain Gypsy Cafe
Rossland, BC

"Caribou is best served rare or medium rare to maintain moisture."

Caribou, Venison OR Elk chops	12	12
Seeded mustard (dijon)	2-3 tbsp.	30-45 mL
Port	1 cup	250 mL
Beef stock	1 cup	250 mL
Blue cheese (stilton OR danish blue)	1 oz.	30 g

Lightly coat chops in seeded mustard. Let sit for 1 hour.

In a small saucepan, combine port and beef stock. Bring to a boil. Reduce heat to medium and crumble in cheese. Whisk to dissolve cheese. Set aside.

Grill or pan-fry chops for approximately 4 minutes each side, or until cooked to desired preference. Heat sauce and pour over chops. Serve with vegetables and roast potatoes.

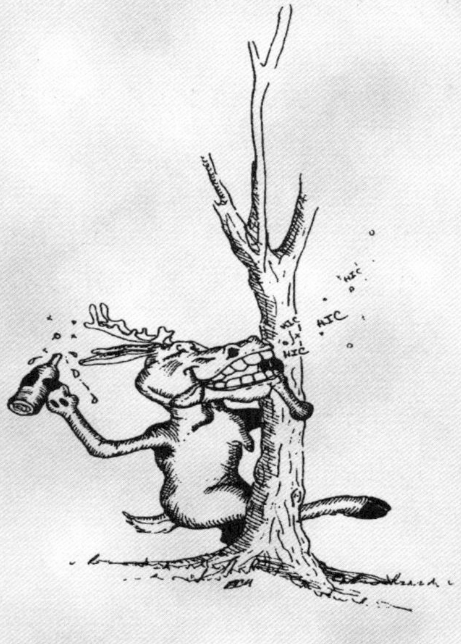

Moose Roast with Veggies

Hazel Calder
New Denver, BC

A nutritional meal all in one pot.

Moose roast	3 lbs.	1.5 kg
Flour	1/3 cup	75 mL
Oil	2 tbsp.	30 mL
Salt	2 tsp.	10 mL
Pepper, to taste		
Carrots, sliced	6	6
Potatoes, halved	6	6
Onions, sliced	6	6
Turnips, quartered	6	6

Dredge roast in flour.

In a heavy pot or roaster, heat oil till hot. Add roast and brown on all sides. Sprinkle with salt and pepper. Add a little water to prevent burning. Bake in 300°F (150°C) oven for 2 hours.

Put vegetables with meat and bake another 1/2 hour , or until vegetables are tender. Remove meat and vegetables to warmed platter. Use pan drippings for a wonderful gravy.

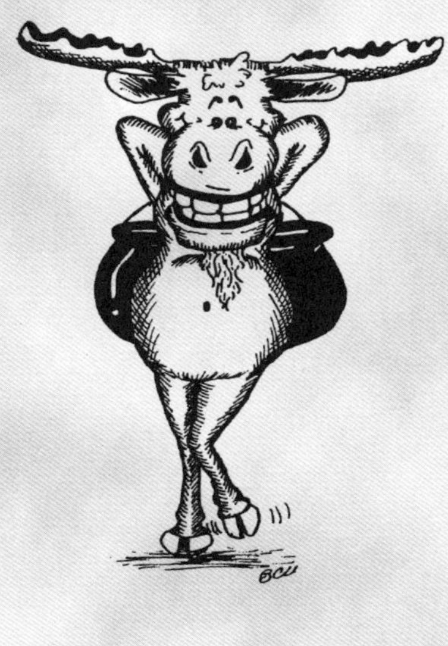

Prize Winning Bombay Shrimp

Heather's Kitchen
Rock Creek, BC

"This recipe has won a Vancouver weekly, monthly and yearly award." Congratulations!

Butter OR margarine	3 tbsp.	45 mL
Boiling water	1 cup	250 mL
Flour	3 tbsp.	45 mL
Salt, to taste		
Pepper, to taste		
Evaporated milk	14 oz.	398 mL
Curry powder	2 tbsp.	30 mL
Shrimp (fresh, frozen OR canned)	1 1/2 cups	375 mL

Melt butter in saucepan. Stir in water, flour, salt and pepper. Bring to a boil, stirring constantly. Add milk and curry powder. Reduce heat and simmer 5 minutes. Add shrimp. Remove from heat and let sit for 5 minutes before serving. The shrimp will cook while sitting in curry sauce.

Serve over steamed rice to which 1/4 cup (60 mL) pimiento has been added.

Variation: Substitute shrimp with same quantity of crab, pollock or canned salmon.

DID YOU KNOW... In buying, remember, 2 lbs. (1 kg) of shrimp in the shell gives only about 1 lb. (500 g) cooked, shelled shrimp, or 2 cups (500 mL).

Special Chicken Fettuccine

Special... need I say more?

Olive oil	2-3 tbsp.	30-45 mL
Medium onion, chopped	1	1
Garlic cloves, crushed	2	2
Mushrooms, quartered	2 cups	500 mL
Salt	1/2 tsp.	2 mL
Pepper	1/4 tsp.	1 mL
Chicken breast, bite size pieces	2	2
Garlic cloves, crushed	2	2
Fettuccine noodles	8 oz.	250 g
Grated parmesan cheese	1/2 cup	125 mL
Egg	1	1
Light cream OR whipping cream	3 tbsp.	45 mL
Grated parmesan cheese, sprinkle		

Heat olive oil in large skillet. Sauté onion and garlic until slightly browned. Add mushrooms, salt and pepper and sauté until soft. Remove from skillet. Set aside.

Heat oiled skillet, adding chicken and remaining garlic. Cook until tender.

Cook fettuccine according to package directions until tender but firm. Drain. Add to chicken. Alternate adding mushroom mixture and first amount of parmesan cheese. Toss after each addition. Slowly add beaten egg. Stir until egg has cooked. Mix in cream. Turn out onto serving platter or into bowl. Sprinkle with remaining parmesan cheese. Serves 4-6.

Variniki

Shirley Relkoff
Winlaw, BC

"This traditional Doukhobor dish has been originally served on New Years Day however, they are enjoyed as often as they are made... which is often."

DOUGH:

Recipe #1

Flour	4 cups	1 L
Baking powder	1 tsp.	5 mL
Baking soda	1 tsp.	5 mL
Salt	1 tsp.	5 mL
Sour cream	2 cups	500 mL
Eggs, beaten	2	2

Recipe #2

Flour	2 1/2 cups	625 mL
Baking powder	1/2 tsp.	2 mL
Baking soda	1/4 tsp.	1 mL
Salt	1 tsp.	5 mL
Buttermilk	1 cup	250 mL
Oil	1 tbsp.	15 mL
Eggs	2	2

FILLINGS:

Cottage cheese filling:

Dry cottage cheese	3 cups	750 mL
Salt	1 tsp.	5 mL
Eggs	2	2

Potato filling:

Mashed potatoes	3 cups	750 mL

Variniki Continued...

Egg	1	1
Grated cheddar cheese (optional)	$^{1}/_{2}$ cup	125 mL
Salt, to taste		

Instructions:

Recipe #1

In a large bowl, stir flour, baking powder, soda and salt. Make a well in the center.

In a separate bowl, mix together sour cream and eggs. Pour into well. Mix dough until combined. Turn dough out onto well floured surface and knead until soft dough forms. Roll dough to thickness of pie crust. Cut into $2^{1}/_{2}$ inch (6 cm) circles.

Recipe #2

Combine flour, baking powder, soda and salt in a large bowl. Make a well in the center.

In a separate bowl, mix together buttermilk, oil and eggs. Pour into well. Mix dough until combined. Turn dough out onto well floured surface and knead until soft dough forms. Roll dough to thickness of pie crust. Cut into $2^{1}/_{2}$ inch (6 cm) circles.

Desired Fillings:

In a bowl, mix together ingredients of selected filling.

Fill circles with 1 tsp. (5 mL) of filling. Pinch edges together to close. Drop into pot of 8 cups (2 L) boiling salted water. Return to a boil and cook 4 minutes. Remove and put in bowl. Add melted butter to prevent sticking. Serve with sour cream and butter.

Bubbalu's Classic Fettuccine Alfredo

Allen Sorenson
Windsor Hotel
Trout Lake, BC

"Serve with garlic toast and garnish with finely diced tomato, green onion and sprinkled parmesan cheese. Serves 3 hungry Italians."

Butter OR margarine	2 tbsp.	30 mL
Virgin olive oil	1 tbsp.	15 mL
Fresh ground garlic	1 tsp.	5 mL
Mushrooms, quartered	8	8
Carrots, julienne	1/3 cup	75 mL
Green peppers, julienne	1/3 cup	75 mL
Small onion, slivered	1/4 cup	60 mL
Ham, diced (optional)	1/3 cup	75 mL
Chicken soup base	2 tsp.	10 mL
Tarragon, pinch		
Basil, pinch		
Oregano, pinch		
Salt and pepper, pinch		
Whipping cream	1 3/4 cups	400 mL
Fettuccine noodles, cooked	8 oz.	250 g
Parmesan cheese	1/4 cup	60 mL
Cooked peas	1/4 cup	60 mL
Broccoli heads, blanched	1/4 cup	60 mL

In large frying pan, heat butter, oil and garlic.

Add and sauté mushrooms, carrots, green peppers, onion and ham till vegetables are tender.

Bubbalu's Classic Fettuccine Alfredo Continued...

Season with soup base, tarragon, basil, oregano, salt and pepper. Stir in whipping cream and reduce to medium heat.

Add cooked fettuccine noodles and parmesan cheese. Stir until well mixed. Add peas and broccoli. Reduce heat and stir till thickness of sauce is desired. Season to taste.

Pictured on page 89.

Sheila's Rice Casserole

Isabel Snelgrove
Crawford Bay, BC

Quick and easy!

Regular rice	2 cups	500 mL
Soya sauce	1/4 cup	60 mL
Boiling water	3 cups	750 mL
Packaged onion soup mix	1	1
Vegetable oil	1/4 cup	60 mL
Canned peas, drained	10 oz.	284 mL
Sliced mushrooms, drained	10 oz.	284 mL
Cooked meats (optional)		

Combine all ingredients in a 2-quart (2 L) casserole dish. Cover and bake in 350°F (175° C) oven for 1- 1 1/2 hours. Serves 4-6.

DID YOU KNOW... When preparing white rice, the rice will be fluffier and whiter if you add 1 tsp. (5 mL) lemon juice to each 1 quart (1 L) of water.

Barley Pilaf

Dreana Ratcliffe
Nakusp, BC

A nice change from rice.

Chicken broth	2 cups	500 mL
Butter OR margarine	1/4 cup	60 mL
Salt and pepper, to taste		
Small onion	1	1
Green pepper, chopped	1/4 cup	60 mL
Fresh mushrooms, sliced	3 cups	750 mL
Barley	1 cup	250 mL
Large garlic cloves, crushed	3	3

In medium saucepan, bring chicken broth, butter, salt and pepper to a boil. Stir in onion, green pepper, mushrooms, barley and garlic. Reduce heat to medium low, cover and simmer for 30-40 minutes. If it dries out, add a little water. Good hot or cold. Serves 4-6.

DID YOU KNOW... Fruit trees that were planted in the late 1800's by Rosslands Chinese community of 200 men and 1 woman, still produce fruit today.

Bubbalu's Classic Fettuccine Alfredo, page 86
Country Apple Crisp, page 118
Batter Buns, page 94
Spinach Salad, page 39
Cheesy Corn Chowder, page 23
Borscht in Dutch Oven, page 27

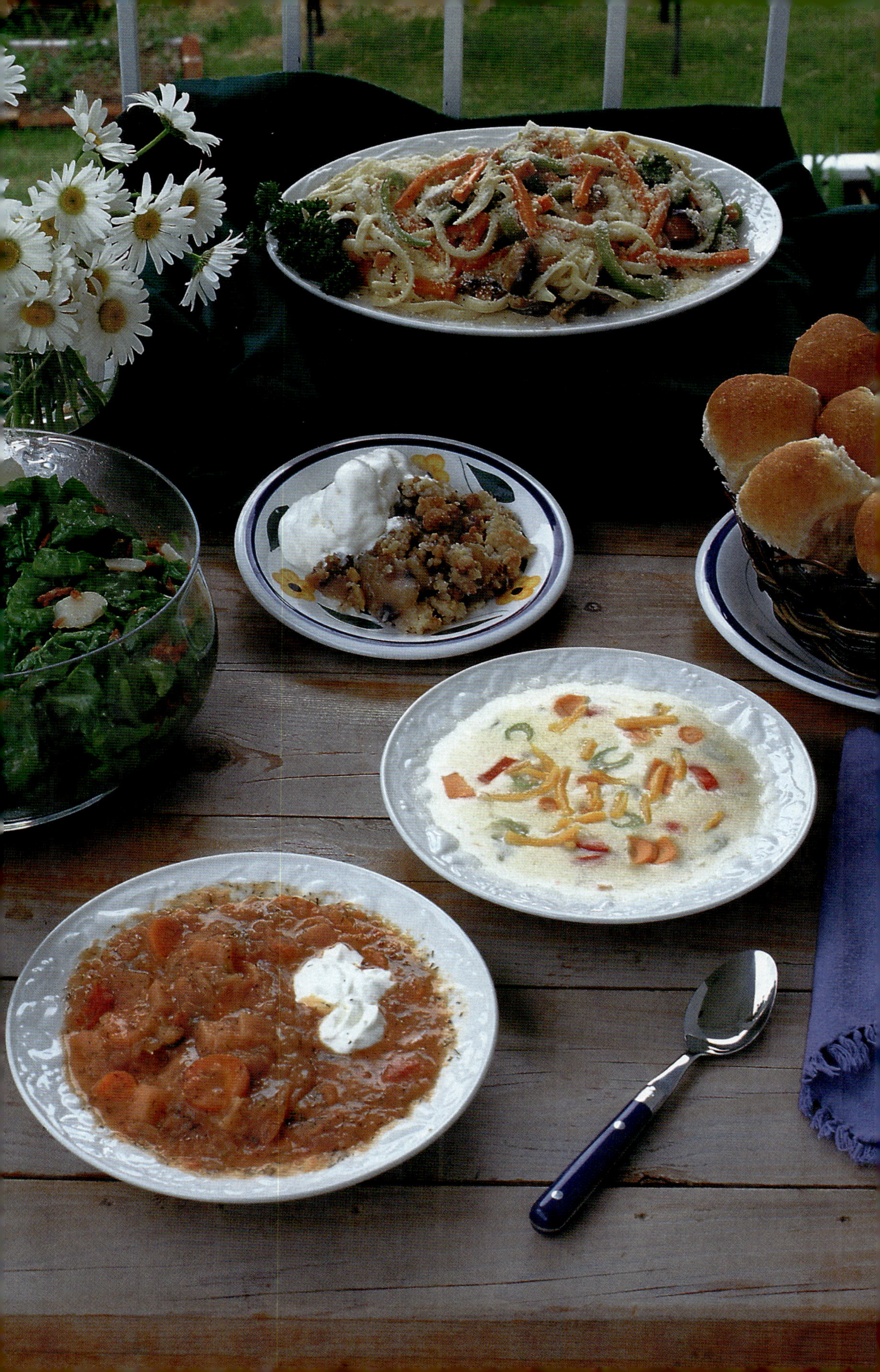

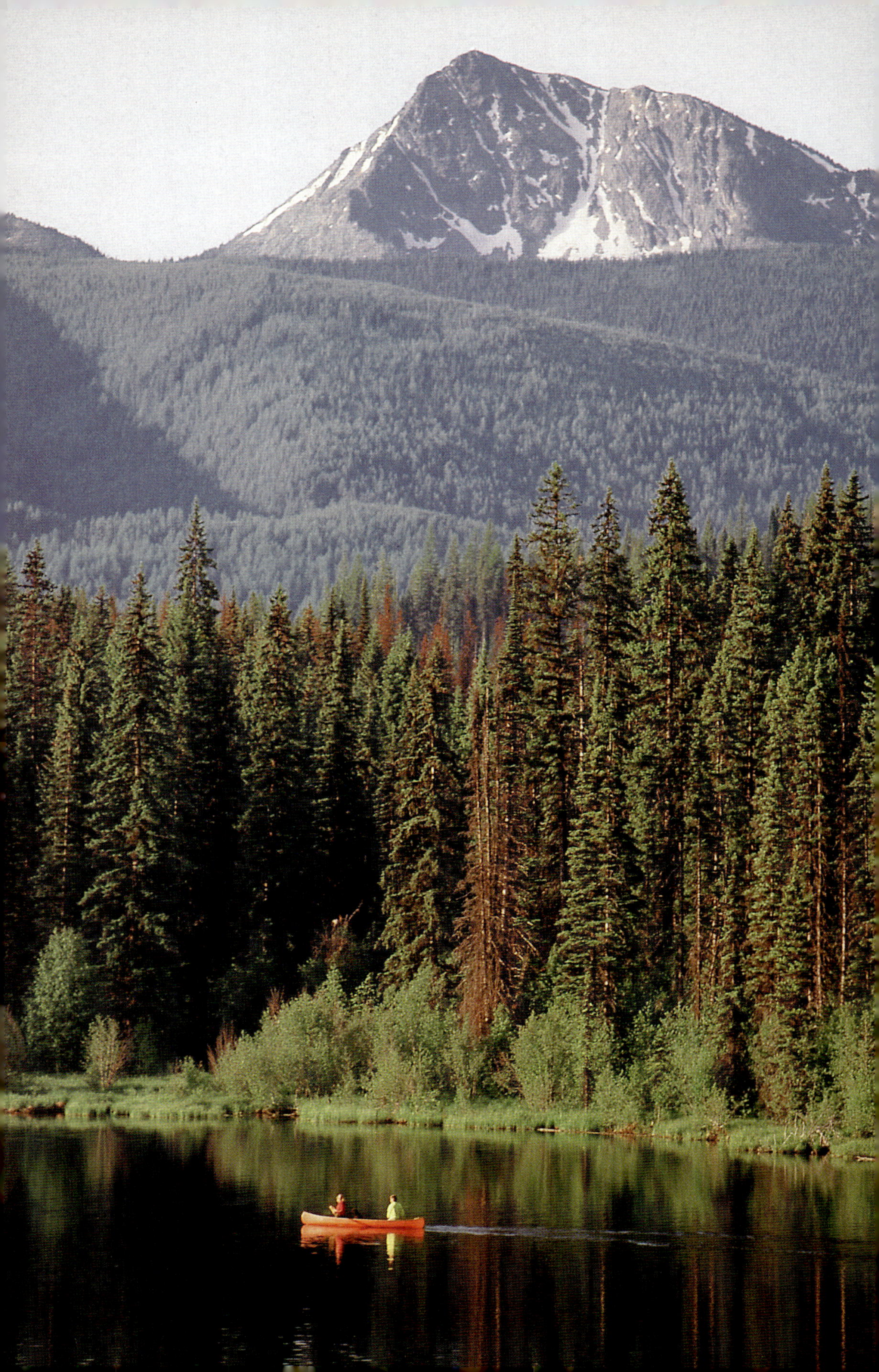

Carol's Pesto of the "Firs"

Hazel Calder
New Denver, BC

Pesto is a wonderful sauce used in pasta, vegetables and salad recipes.

Fresh basil, leaves only	2 cups	500 mL
Grated Parmesan cheese	1 cup	250 mL
Olive oil	1 cup	250 mL
Roasted pine nuts	1/2 cup	125 mL
Garlic cloves	6	6

In a blender or food processor, puree basil, parmesan cheese, olive oil, pine nuts and garlic together. Divide into 1/3 cup (75 mL) to 1/2 cup (125 mL) portions into zip lock bags, small jars, or ice cube trays (freeze in trays and transfer into zip lock bag). Store in freezer. Thaw before usage. If not freezing, add layer of olive oil to each jar to keep pesto from darkening. Refrigerate for up to 1 week.

Variation: Substitute 2 cups (500 mL) fresh basil with 1/2 cup (125 mL) dried basil.

PESTO IDEAS:
Pasta with Pesto - To 4 cups (1 L) hot pasta, add 5-6 tbsp. (75-90 mL) basil pesto and 1 cup (250 mL) grated parmesan cheese. Serves 4-6.

Pesto Butter - Blend 3 tbsp. (45 mL) basil pesto with 1/2 cup (125 mL) butter.

Pesto Dressing- Blend 6 tbsp. (90 mL) basil pesto with 1/3 cup (75 mL) wine vinegar, 2/3 cup (150 mL) olive oil and 1 crushed garlic clove.

Canoeing on the Nancy Green Lake with
Old Glory Mountain in the background.

The Family Lasagne

Kelley Buckley
Nakusp, BC

"A traditional pasta dish. A meal that freezes well."

Ground beef, lean	1 lb.	500 g
Canned tomatoes	16 oz.	500 g
Canned tomato paste	12 oz.	355 mL
Garlic powder	1/8 tsp.	0.5 mL
Basil	1 tbsp.	15 mL
Salt	1 1/2 tsp.	7 mL
Creamy cottage cheese	3 cups	750 mL
Grated Parmesan cheese	1/2 cup	125 mL
Parsley flakes	2 tbsp.	30 mL
Eggs	2	2
Salt	1 tsp.	5 mL
Pepper	1/2 tsp.	2 mL
Lasagne noodles, cooked and drained	8-10	8-10
Mozzarella cheese, grated	2 cups	500 mL

In a large frying pan, brown ground beef. Drain. Add tomatoes, tomato paste, garlic powder, basil and salt. Mix well. Simmer uncovered for 30 minutes, stir occasionally.

In a bowl, mix together cottage cheese, Parmesan cheese, parsley, eggs, salt and pepper.

In a 9 x 13 inch (22 x 33 cm) pan, assemble mixtures in following layers: 1/2 noodles; 1/2 cottage cheese mixture; 1/2 mozzarella cheese; 1/2 meat sauce. Repeat layers. Add additional cheese to the top layer. Bake in 350°F (175°C) oven for 40 minutes. Let sit for 5 minutes before cutting. Serves 8-12.

Garlic Toast Topping

Dreana Ratcliffe
Nakusp, BC

A delicious spread for your favorite bread or bun. Serve with salad, pasta or soup.

Garlic cloves, crushed	12	12
Vegetable oil	3/4 cup	175 mL
Whipping cream	1 1/2 cups	375 mL
Grated parmesan cheese	1 cup	250 mL
Butter OR margarine, melted	3 tbsp.	45 mL
Paprika	1/2 tsp.	2 mL

Bread OR buns of choice

In a bowl or blender, whip together all 6 ingredients until thick and creamy. Spread on bread or buns. Broil until bubbly and brown, 3-5 minutes. Store spread in refrigerator.

Pictured on page 35.

DID YOU KNOW... Peel garlic and store in a covered jar of vegetable oil. The garlic will stay fresh and the oil will be nicely flavored for salad dressings.

Batter Buns

Marcy Nixon
Nakusp, BC

The seniors at Halcyon Home in Nakusp enjoy the aroma of these buns baking.

Active dry yeast	1 tbsp.	15 mL
Warm water	1 cup	250 mL
Sugar	2 tbsp.	30 mL
Salt	1 tsp.	5 mL
Large egg	1	1
Shortening	2 tbsp.	30 mL
Flour	2 1/4 cups	550 mL

In a large bowl, dissolve yeast in warm water and let stand for 10 minutes.

Beat sugar, salt, egg, shortening and 1 cup of the flour into yeast mixture. Beat until smooth. Beat in remaining flour until well mixed. Cover and let rise 30 minutes.

Stir down batter. Fill greased muffin tins 1/2 to 2/3 full. Let rise for another 30 minutes. Bake in a 400°F (205°C) oven for 15 minutes. Makes 10-12 buns

Variation: If you prefer a "dinner bun", add 1 cup flour, knead, shape buns. Bake on greased cookie sheet or in greased 9 x 13 inch (22 x 33 cm) baking pan.

Pictured on page 71, 89, and 107.

DID YOU KNOW... For vitamin packed breads, you can use potato water to replace exact amounts of water. Store potato water in the fridge for later use.

Mark's Whole Wheat Bread

Mark Shubin
Crawford Bay, BC

Mark's secret to successful bread is the kneading process. He is convinced that kneading this bread 700 times (give or take a couple hundred) produces great tasting home made fresh bread.

Whole wheat flour	12 cups	3 L
Instant yeast	2 tbsp.	30 mL
Salt	2 tbsp.	30 mL
Assorted seeds: (sunflower, millet, flax)	1 cup	250 mL
Warm apple herb tea	4 1/2 cups	1.125 L
Oil	1/4 cup	60 mL
Honey	1/4 cup	60 mL
Lemon juice	2 tbsp.	30 mL
Molasses	1/4 cup	60 mL

Combine flour, yeast, salt and assorted seeds together in large bowl. Make well in center.

In a separate bowl, mix remaining 5 wet ingredients together. Pour into well. Combine to form dough. Turn out on floured surface and knead until soft dough forms. Put into greased bowl, cover and let rise 2 hours. Punch down, cover and let rise for additional 1 hour. Roll dough out flat to remove air bubbles. Cut dough in four, shape into loaves, and place the loaves in 4 well greased 9 x 5 inch (23 x 13 cm) loaf pans. Lightly cut tops diagonally and sprinkle on dash of flour. Cover and let rise until doubled, 1 hour. Bake in 425°F (220°C) oven for 10 minutes. Reduce heat to 325°F (160°C) and bake for additional 30 minutes. Remove loaves from pans and let cool on oven rack. Once cool, eat, bag and/or freeze. Do not store in refrigerator. Makes 4 loaves.

Pictured on page 107.

Dill Bread

Betsy-Ann Gallinger
Crawford Bay, BC

A light textured bread.

Active dry yeast	1 tbsp.	15 mL
Warm water	1/4 cup	60 mL
Cottage cheese	1 cup	250 mL
Dill weed	2 tsp.	10 mL
Salt	1 1/2 tsp.	7 mL
Baking soda	1/4 tsp.	1 mL
Egg	1	1
Butter OR margarine, melted	1 tbsp.	15 mL
Onion, minced	1 1/2 tsp.	7 mL
Sugar	1 tbsp.	15 mL
Flour	2 1/4 cups	550mL

In a small bowl, dissolve yeast in water. Set aside.

In a large bowl, combine cottage cheese, dill weed, salt, baking soda, egg, butter, onion and sugar. Stir in yeast mixture. Add flour stirring until well blended. Turn out on floured surface and knead for 5-10 minutes until soft dough forms. Add more flour if needed. Put in greased bowl, cover and let rise till doubled in size, about 1 hour. Punch down. Divide dough in half and place in two greased 9 x 5 inch (23 x 12 cm) loaf pans. Cover and let rise for another 45 minutes. Bake in 350°F (180°C) oven for 30 minutes. Remove from pans and brush with melted butter. Makes 2 loaves.

Pictured on page 107.

Hop Sing's Outrageous Yorkshire Pudding

Allen Sorensen
Windsor Hotel
Trout Lake, BC

"The results of great Yorkshire is not in the ingredients, but simply in the method applied. Your oil must be hot and smoking, as well as the mixture must be cool! When these two are combined, and your time is watched accordingly, you've got yourselves some outrageous Yorkshire."

Eggs	3	3
Flour	1 cup	250 mL
Chicken soup base	1 tbsp.	15 mL
Milk	1 1/3 cups	325 mL
Vegetable oil OR Virgin olive oil	1/4 cup	60 mL

Make sure all ingredients are at room temperature.

In a bowl mix eggs, flour and chicken soup base together. Add milk and whisk until mixture is smooth. Refrigerate.

Fill muffin pan (for six) 1/4 inch (0.5 cm) full with oil. Place on cookie sheet (to prevent spillage from burning). Heat in 500°F (260°C) until oil is smoking hot!

Mix batter again. Fill hot oiled pans 3/4 inch (2 cm) full. Bake in 500°F (260°C) oven for 25 minutes. Reduce heat to 300°F (150°C) and bake another 10 minutes. Reduce heat to 100°F (40°C) and bake for last 20 minutes.

Remove from oven and serve with your favorite beef. Makes 6 yorkshire puddings.

Dropped Doughnuts

Nancy Savage
Trout Lake, BC

"Great for lunchboxes. Enjoy!"

Flour	1½ cups	375 mL
Sugar	½ cup	125 mL
Baking powder	2 tsp.	10 mL
Salt	¼ tsp.	1 mL
Nutmeg	¼ tsp.	1 mL
Grated rind of lemon	1	1
Milk	½ cup	125 mL
Egg, beaten	1	1

Shortening OR cooking oil

Sugar, to taste
Cinnamon, to taste

In a bowl, mix together first 8 ingredients until soft dough is formed. Dough should be soft but not liquid.

Carefully drop by teaspoon into hot oil. Hold spoon close to pan to prevent splatters. Doughnuts will rise to top. Remove when light brown color. Shake in bag with sugar or a mixture of sugar and cinnamon.

Variation: You may add small pieces of fresh fruit to batter.

Pictured on page 143.

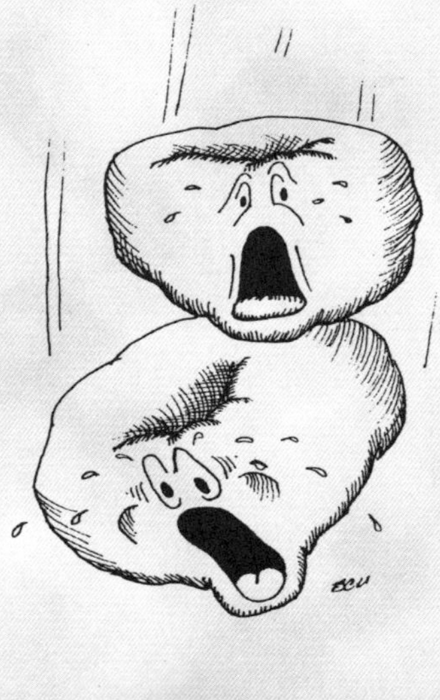

Gooey Buns

Blaire Buckley
Nakusp, BC

This is a great morning saver when you have overnight company. You'll "wow" them at breakfast.

Pecans	1 cup	250 mL
Frozen doughballs	18	18
Cinnamon	4 tbsp.	60 mL
Butterscotch pudding (NOT instant)	6 oz.	170 g
Butter OR margarine	1/2 cup	125 mL
Brown sugar	1 cup	250 mL

Place pecans in bottom of well greased bundt or angel food cake pan. Place frozen doughballs in bottom of pan. Sprinkle cinnamon and butterscotch pudding powder on top.

In a saucepan, melt butter. Remove from heat and stir in brown sugar. Pour over dough balls. Cover and let rise overnight. Bake in 350°F (175°C) oven for 30 minutes. Enjoy!

What are frozen doughballs? They are frozen white roll (bun) dough. You can find them in the frozen section of your supermarket.

Pictured on page 107.

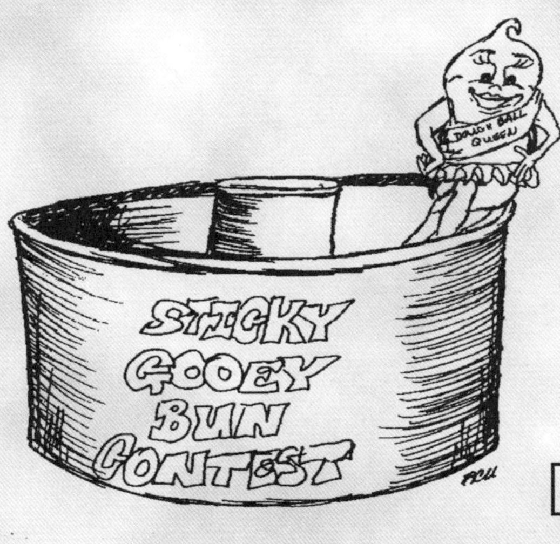

Oats 'n' Apple Breakfast

Kim Fuzzen
Crawford Bay, BC

You prepare this delightful breakfast cereal the night before serving. This breakfast is not only delicious, but full of nutrition.

Hulled oats	3 1/2 cups	825 mL
Raisins	1 cup	250 mL
Almonds	1 cup	250 mL
Apples, peeled and sliced	2	2
Cinnamon, dash		

Cover oats, raisins and almonds with water. Soak overnight.

In the morning, drain oat mixture. Grind together with freshly sliced apples and cinnamon. May serve with milk, or is delicious by itself. Serves 4-6.

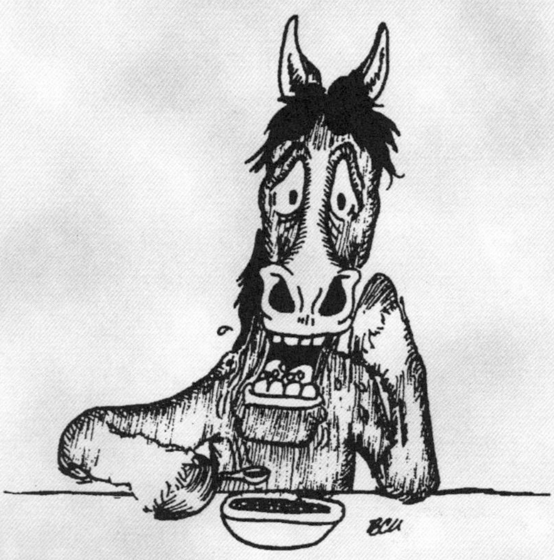

DID YOU KNOW... Whole grain oats contain seven B vitamins, vitamin E, and nine minerals, including iron and calcium. The protein content and quality of that protein is superior to that of wheat and most other grains.

Country Granola

Hornby Family
Nakusp, BC

"This recipe can be cut in half but it freezes so well, it's well worth making a large batch. Can be eaten as a breakfast cereal with milk or sprinkled on top of your favorite cereal or yogurt for added fiber."

Rolled oats, large flake	16 cups	4 L
Unsweetened coconut, shredded	3 cups	750 mL
Natural bran	2 cups	500 mL
Wheat germ	1 cup	250 mL
Sliced almonds	1 cup	250 mL
Sunflower seeds, unsalted	1 cup	250 mL
Pumpkin seeds, unsalted	1/2 cup	125 mL
Unsalted cashews, chopped	1 cup	250 mL
Honey	2 cups	500 mL
Raisins	3 cups	750 mL
Dried apricots, OR papaya OR combination	2 cups	500 mL

Mix first 8 ingredients thoroughly in large bowl.

In saucepan melt honey until liquid. Toss into dry ingredients until well coated. Pour 1/3 mixture onto two ungreased baking sheets. Toast in 275°F (140°C) oven for 7 minutes. Remove from oven, gently turn mixture over and toast another 5 minutes until dry. Transfer into another large bowl. Continue process until remaining mixture is toasted.

Stir in raisins and apricots. Cool. Store in airtight containers in fridge or freezer.

Variation: Substitute 1 cup (250 mL) honey with 1 cup (250 mL) dark corn syrup.

Pictured on page 143.

Favorite Lemon Loaf

Pat Munroe
Salmo, BC

For the lemon lovers.

Butter, margarine OR shortening	1/2 cup	125 mL
Sugar	1 cup	250 mL
Eggs	2	2
Milk	1/2 cup	125 mL
Flour	1 1/2 cups	375 mL
Baking powder	1 tsp.	5 mL
Salt	1/2 tsp.	2 mL
Grated rind of lemon		
GLAZE:		
Juice of lemon	1	1
Sugar	1/4 cup	60 mL

In large bowl, cream butter and sugar. Add eggs one at a time beating until creamy. Blend in milk.

In another bowl, mix together flour, baking powder, salt and lemon rind. Pour into batter. Stir to moisten. Scrape into greased 9 x 5 inch (23 x 13 cm) loaf pan. Bake in 350°F (180°C) oven for 55-60 minutes. Spoon glaze evenly over top of hot loaf. Cool. Makes 1 loaf.

GLAZE:
Combine lemon juice and sugar in saucepan. Stir and heat till sugar is dissolved. Spoon evenly over top of hot loaf. Cool. Makes 1 loaf.

Pictured on page 143.

Like No Other Zucchini Loaf

Wayne Schweitzer
Nelson, BC

A loaf to take pride in. Scrumptious!

Brown OR golden sugar	1 cup	250 mL
White sugar	1 cup	250 mL
Vegetable oil	1 cup	250 mL
Eggs	3	3
Vanilla extract	1 tsp.	5 mL
Raw zucchini, grated	2 cups	500 mL
Mapleine flavoring	2 tsp.	10 mL
Flour	3 cups	750 mL
Baking soda	1 tsp.	5 mL
Salt	1-2 tsp.	5-10 mL
Baking powder	1/4 tsp.	1 mL
Cinnamon	1 1/2 tbsp.	22 mL
Raisins OR chopped walnuts	1 1/4 cups	300 mL

In a bowl, beat together first 7 ingredients until smooth and well blended.

Sift next 5 dry ingredients together in another bowl. Beat into batter. Stir in raisins or walnuts. Pour into two greased 9 x 5 inch (23 x 13 cm) loaf pans and bake in 375°F (190°C) oven for 1 hour. Test with toothpick. Let stand for 10 minutes before removing from pan to cool on rack. Yield: 2 loaves.

DID YOU KNOW... Nelson is the sight of such films as "Roxanne", "Housekeeping" and "Gold Digger".

Best Ever Scones

Elsie Giberson
Nakusp, BC

"This recipe originated in Revelstoke where men working on Rotary snow plows always packed some in their lunch. Also used to give quick energy to hardworking railroad men."

Flour	2 cups	500 mL
Sugar	2 tbsp.	30 mL
Baking powder	2 tsp.	10 mL
Baking soda	3/4 tsp.	4 mL
Salt	3/4 tsp.	4 mL
Butter OR margarine	1/2 cup	125 mL
Raisins or blueberries	2/3 cup	150 mL
Egg	1	1
Buttermilk	2/3 cup	150 mL

Mix first 5 ingredients together in large bowl. Cut in butter until crumbly. Stir in raisins or blueberries. Make a well in center.

In a small bowl, beat egg until frothy. Stir in buttermilk. Pour into well. Stir with a fork to form soft dough. Turn out on lightly floured surface. Knead 8-10 times. Pat or roll 3/4 inch (2 cm) thick circle. Cut into wedges. Place on greased cookie sheet. Bake in 350°F (175°C) oven for 15 minutes or until lightly browned edges. Makes 14-16 scones

Pictured on page 107.

DID YOU KNOW... A piece of celery in your bread bag will keep the bread fresh for a longer time.

Ginger Orange Scones

Jenny Shkurhan
Wynndel, BC

These are great served warm or cold.

Flour	3 cups	750 mL
Brown sugar	1/4 cup	60 mL
Baking powder	2 tsp.	10 mL
Baking soda	1 tsp.	5 mL
Cream of tartar	1 tsp.	5 mL
Salt	1/2 tsp.	2 mL
Ground ginger	2 tsp.	10 mL
Crystallized ginger, finely chopped	1/4 cup	60 mL
Butter OR margarine	1/3 cup	75 mL
Grated orange rind	1/2 tsp.	2 mL
Buttermilk	1 1/3 cups	325 mL

In a large bowl, combine first 8 ingredients. Cut in margarine until crumbly.

Mix orange rind and buttermilk together. Add to dry mixture. Stir until soft dough is formed. Turn out on lightly floured surface. Knead 8-10 times. Divide dough in half. Roll or pat each portion into 1/2 to 3/4 inch (2 cm) thick circles. Cut each circle into 8 wedges. Place wedges on cookie sheet 1/2 inch (1.25 cm) apart. Bake in 400°F (205°C) oven for 12 minutes.

Variation: Grated orange rind may be substituted with 1 tbsp. (15 mL) frozen concentrated orange juice or 1/4 cup (60 mL) reconstituted orange juice. If using reconstituted orange juice, use 1/4 cup (60 mL) less buttermilk. Makes 16 scones.

Pictured on page 107.

Prized Carrot Loaf

Lyn Arikado
Nakusp, BC

"This loaf is a cross between a rich bread and a cake."

White sugar	1 cup	250 mL
Vegetable oil	1/2 cup	125 mL
Eggs	2	2
Vanilla	1 tsp.	5 mL
Carrots, grated	1 cup	250 mL
Flour	1 1/2 cups	375 mL
Baking soda	1 tsp.	5 mL
Salt	1/2 tsp.	2 mL
Walnuts, chopped	1/2 cup	125 mL

Beat together sugar, oil, eggs and vanilla in bowl. Stir in carrots. Sift in flour, baking soda, and salt. Mix well. Stir in nuts. Pour into 9 x 5 inch (23 x 13 cm) loaf pan. Bake in 350°F (175°C) oven for 50 minutes. Test with toothpick. Let stand for 10 minutes before removing from pan to cool on rack. Yield: 1 loaf.

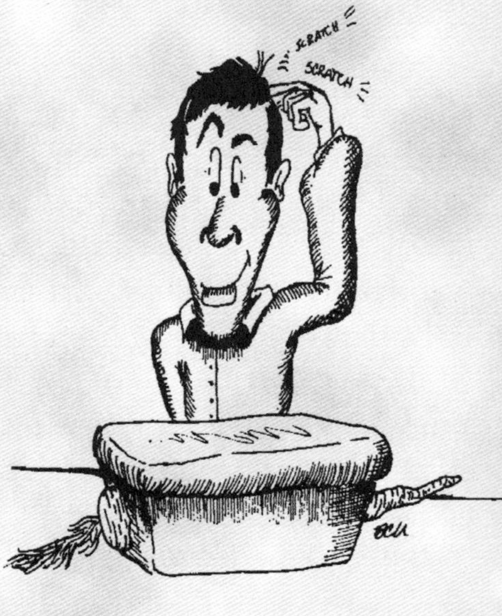

Batter Buns, page 94
Mark's Whole Wheat Bread, page 95
Whipped Raspberry Jam, page 151
Dill Bread, page 96
Gooey Buns, page 99
Best Ever Scones, page 104
Ginger Orange Scones, page 105

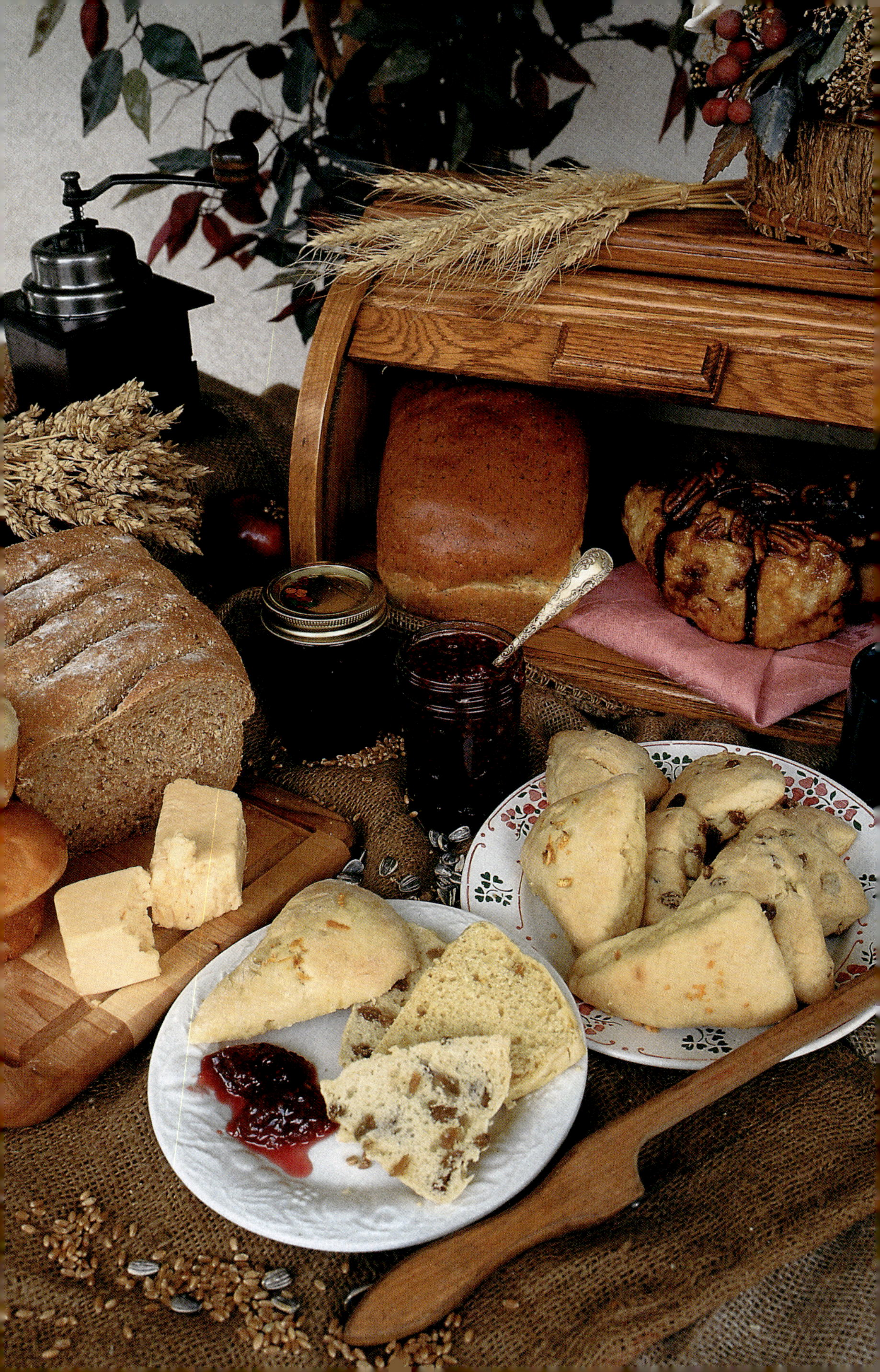

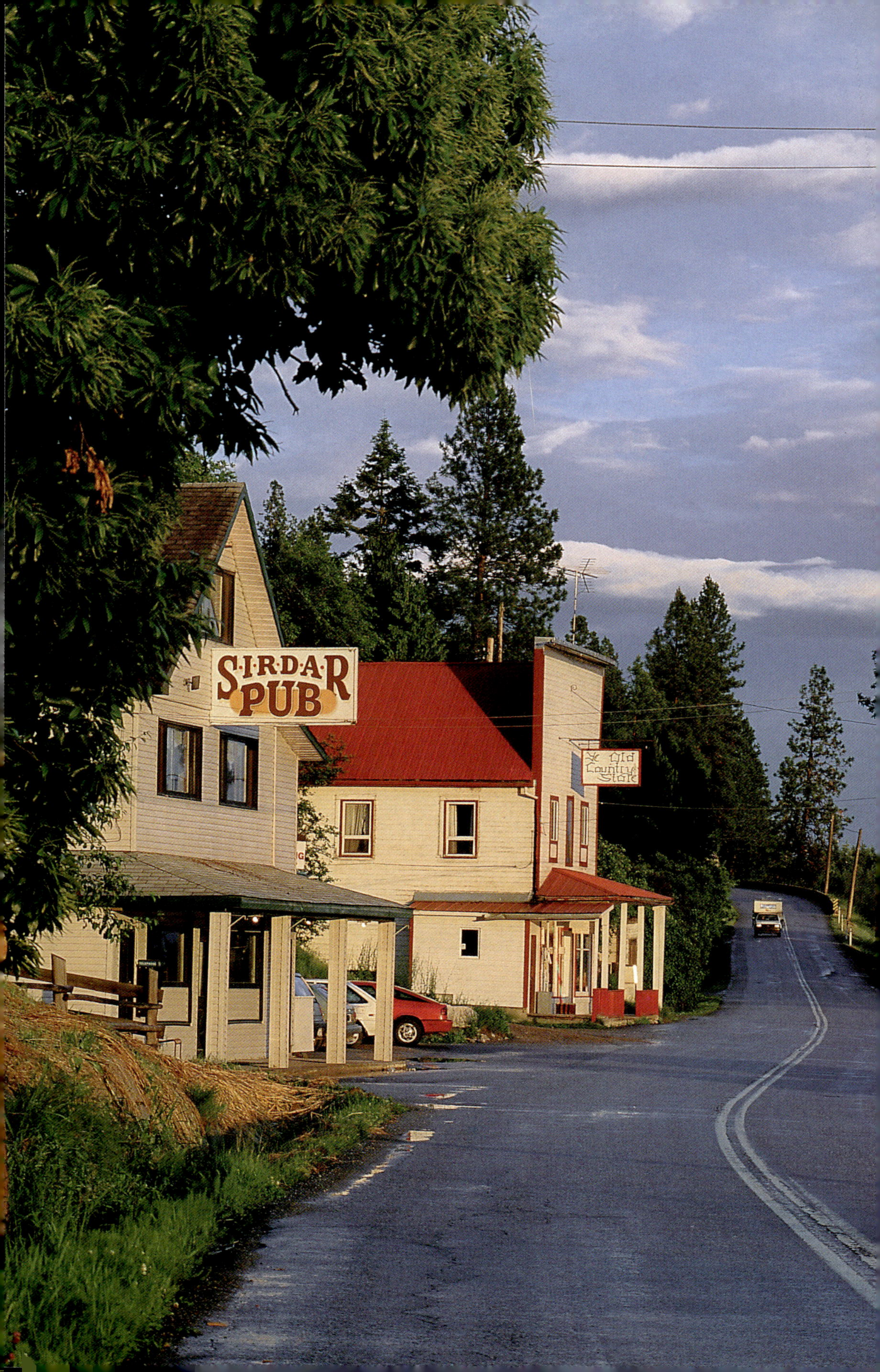
S·I·R·D·A·R
PUB
Ye Old Country Store

Carrot Pineapple Muffins

Dreana Ratcliffe
Nakusp, BC

Moist and delicious.

Flour	1 1/2 cups	375 mL
Sugar	3/4 cup	175 mL
Baking soda	1 tsp.	5 mL
Cinnamon	1 tsp.	5 mL
Salt	1/2 tsp.	2 mL
Baking powder	1 tsp.	5 mL
Eggs	2	2
Oil	2/3 cup	150 mL
Carrots, grated	1 cup	250 mL
Crushed pineapple, undrained	1/2 cup	125 mL
Vanilla	1 tsp.	5 mL

In a large bowl combine all 6 dry ingredients together. Make a well in the center.

Beat eggs until frothy. Mix in oil, carrots, crushed pineapple and vanilla. Pour into well. Stir only to moisten. Fill greased muffin cups 3/4 full. Bake in 375°F (190°C) oven for 20-25 minutes. Let stand 5 minutes before removing from pan. Makes 16.

Pictured on page 143.

Rural buildings at Sirdar, north of Creston.

M.J's Sunshine Muffins

Isabel Snelgrove
Crawford Bay, BC

A bright orange flavored muffin.

Flour	1 1/2 cups	175 mL
Sugar	3/4 cup	375 mL
Baking powder	1 tsp.	5 mL
Baking soda	1 tsp.	5 mL
Salt	1 tsp.	5 mL
Walnuts, chopped	1/2 cup	125 mL
Orange, rind	1	1
Orange juice	1/2 cup	125 mL
Egg	1	1
Oil	1/4 cup	60 mL

Measure first 6 ingredients together in large bowl. Stir together. Make a well in the center.

Cut orange rind into 8 pieces. Blend with juice, egg and oil in blender. Puree and pour into well. Stir just to moisten. Fill greased muffin tins 3/4 full. Bake in 375°F (190°C) for 15-20 minutes. Makes 12 muffins.

Variation: Substitute walnuts with raisins.

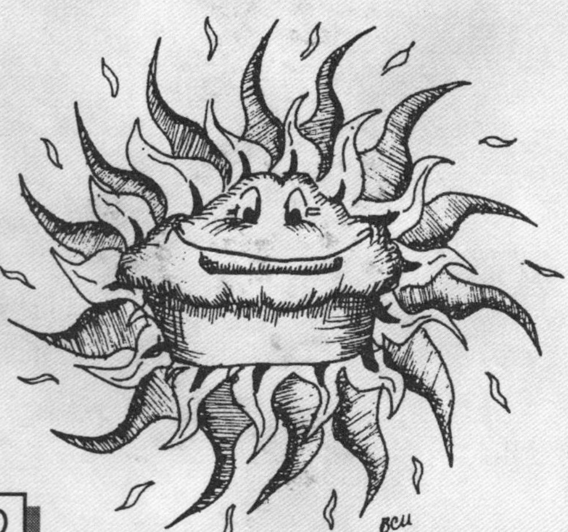

Huckleberry Muffins

Lyn Arikado
Nakusp, BC

A great morning muffin.

Flour	2 cups	500 mL
Baking powder	2 tsp.	10 mL
Salt	1/2 tsp.	2 mL
Butter OR margarine	1/4 cup	60 mL
Icing sugar	1/4 cup	60 mL
Egg yolk, beaten	1	1
Milk	1 cup	250 mL
Egg white	1	1
Huckleberries, fresh	1 cup	250 mL

Reserve 1 tbsp. (15 mL) flour. Sift remaining flour, baking powder, and salt together in bowl.

In a large bowl, cream butter with icing sugar. Add egg yolk and milk. Stir in dry ingredients.

In a small bowl, beat egg white to stiff froth.

Toss huckleberries with reserved flour. Gently fold egg white and huckleberries into batter. Fill greased muffin cups 3/4 full. Bake in 375°F (190°C) oven for 30 minutes, till top is golden brown. Makes 16 muffins.

Variation: Use fresh blueberries instead of huckleberries.

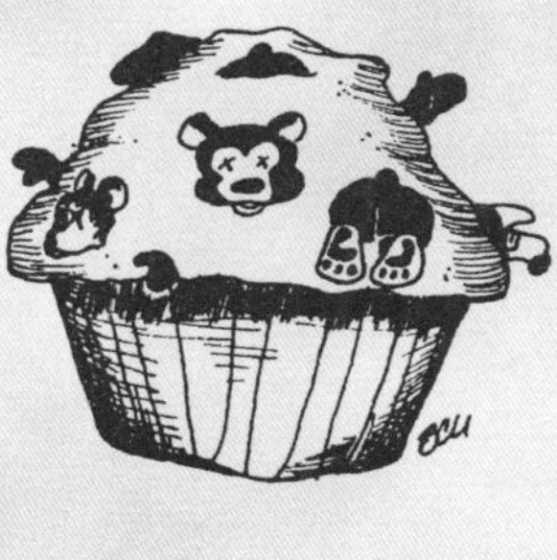

Blueberry Bannock

Hazel Calder
New Denver, BC

"Serve hot with mint tea. Great at a Pow-wow!"

Fresh blueberries Or saskatoons	3 cups	750 mL
Eggs	6	6
Flour	5 cups	1250 mL
Maple OR brown sugar	1 cup	250 mL
Baking powder	4 tsp.	20 mL
Shortening OR oil	3 1/2 cups	825 mL

Press the berries through sieve to obtain 1/2 cup juice. Reserve berries. Beat eggs with juice until creamy. Set aside.

Mix next 3 ingredients together in bowl. Beat egg mixture into dry ingredients. Stir in berries. Drop dough 1 tbsp. (15 mL) at a time into hot oil. Cook until nicely brown. Makes 5 dozen.

Pictured on page 71.

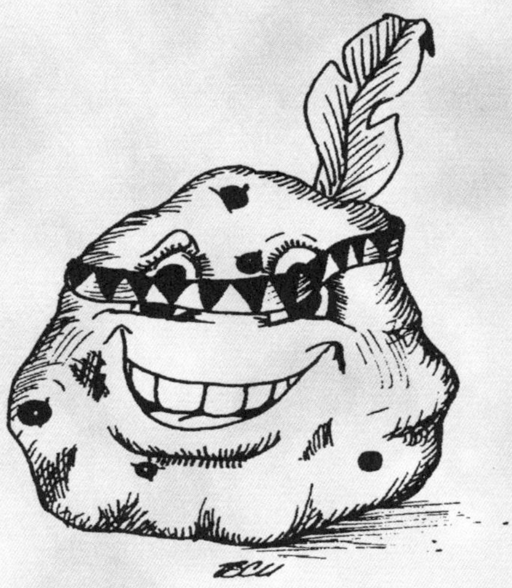

Fruited Madeira Cake

June Brown
Nakusp, BC

The Vancouver Sun has twice awarded this prize winning recipe to June's sister of whom she is very proud.

Seedless raisins	1 cup	250 mL
Currants	1/2 cup	125 mL
Glazed cherries, chopped	1 cup	250 mL
Glazed pineapple rings, chopped	2	2
Flour, sifted	1 3/4 cups	425 mL
Salt	1/2 tsp.	2 mL
Baking powder	1 tsp.	5 mL
Butter OR margarine, softened	2/3 cup	150 mL
Fine sugar	3/4 cup	175 mL
Eggs, beaten	2	2
Milk	1/4 cup	60 mL
Vanilla	1/2 tsp.	2 mL
Almond flavoring	1/2 tsp.	2 mL
Grated rind of orange	1	1
Grated rind of lemon	1	1

Wash and dry raisins and currants. Put in bowl and add cherries and pineapple. Mix in half the flour. In a small bowl, mix together remaining flour, salt and baking powder. Set aside.

Cream butter in large bowl. Gradually beat in sugar and eggs. Add milk, vanilla, almond flavoring, orange rind, lemon rind, floured mixture and floured fruit. Mix well. Spoon into greased 9 x 5 inch (23 x 13 cm) loaf pan. Bake in a 325°F (160°C) oven for 2 hours. Yield: 1 loaf.

Never Fail Jelly Roll

Zerma Alton
Trail, BC

Creativity with fillings makes this marvelous thin sponge cake dessert endless.

Eggs	3	3
Sugar	1 cup	250 mL
Milk	1/2 cup	125 mL
Butter	1 tbsp.	15 mL
Vanilla	1 tsp.	5 mL
All purpose flour OR cake flour	1 cup	250 mL
Baking powder	1 1/2 tbsp.	22 mL
Salt	1/8 tsp.	0.5 mL
Desired jelly OR jam		
Icing sugar		

Beat eggs in large bowl until creamy. Thicken by gradually beating in sugar. Set aside.

In a saucepan, bring milk and butter to boil. Remove from heat.

Add vanilla, flour, baking powder, salt and hot milk to egg mixture. Fold in gently. Pour into wax paper lined or greased 9 x 13 inch (22 x 33 cm) pan and bake in 400°F (205°C) oven for 13-15 minutes.

Immediately, turn out on damp cloth. Cut off crisp edges and spread with jelly or jam. Roll up and sprinkle with icing sugar.

Variation: Omit jelly. About 1 hour before serving, spread chilled whipped cream and 2 cups (500 mL) fresh strawberries on unrolled cake. Roll up; sprinkle with icing sugar and enjoy!

Poppy Seed Chiffon Cake

This cake will not last in your home. Guests always want seconds.

Poppy seeds	1/2 cup	125 mL
Water	1 cup	250 mL
Egg whites	7	7
Cream of tartar	1/2 tsp.	2 mL
Flour	2 cups	500 mL
Baking powder	3 tsp.	15 mL
Sugar	1 1/2 cups	375 mL
Salt	1 tsp.	5 mL
Baking soda	1/4 tsp.	1 mL
Salad oil	1/2 cup	125 mL
Vanilla	2 tsp.	10 mL
Egg yolks	7	7
ICING:		
Soft butter OR margarine	1/2 cup	125 mL
Icing sugar	3/4 cup	175 mL
Light cream	2 tsp.	10 mL
Boiling water	2 tbsp.	30 mL
Almond extract flavoring	1/4 tsp.	1 mL

Soak poppy seeds in water for 2 hours.

In a large bowl, beat egg whites and cream of tartar until very stiff peaks form.

In a separate bowl, sift next 5 dry ingredients together. Form a well and add poppy seed mixture, oil, vanilla and egg yolks. Beat until smooth. Fold into stiffly beaten egg whites. Pour into 10 inch (25 cm) tube pan. Bake in 325°F (160°C) oven for 50 minutes. Increase oven to 350°F (175°C) and bake another 10-15 minutes. Immediately turn pan upside down to cool. Remove cooled cake from pan and spread with whipped icing. Enjoy!

Pictured on page 143.

Cranberry Coffee Cake

Margaret MacDonald
Salmo, BC

With their bitter-sweetness, cranberries in this cake are a treat.

Cream cheese, softened	8 oz.	250 g
White sugar	1 1/2 cups	375 mL
Butter OR margarine	1 cup	250 mL
Vanilla	1 1/2 tsp.	7 mL
Eggs	4	4
Flour	2 1/4 cups	550 mL
Baking powder	1 1/2 tsp.	7 mL
Salt	1/2 tsp.	2 mL
Nutmeg, grated or ground	1/4 tsp.	1 mL
Cranberries	2 1/2 cups	625 mL
Pecans, chopped	1/2 cup	125 mL
Icing sugar	1 tbsp.	15 mL

In a large bowl, beat together cream cheese, sugar, butter and vanilla until smooth. Beat in eggs, one at a time.

In another bowl, stir together 2 cups (500 mL) flour, baking powder, salt and nutmeg. In portions, add into batter, stirring until combined.

Toss together cranberries and pecans in remaining flour. Fold into batter and pour into greased 10 inch (25 cm) bundt pan or angel food pan. Bake in 350°F (175°C) oven for 55-60 minutes, or until toothpick comes out clean. Cool for 15 minutes, then turn onto plate. Dust with icing sugar. Serves 16.

DID YOU KNOW... There are approximately 1192 picnic tables throughout the Kootenay Country.

Strawberry Rhubarb Coffee Cake

Claudette Scott
Nakusp, BC

Fresh OR frozen strawberries, sliced	2 cups	500 mL
Rhubarb, sliced	3 cups	750 mL
Lemon juice	2 tbsp.	30 mL
Sugar	1 cup	250 mL
Cornstarch	1/3 cup	75 mL
Butter OR margarine	1 cup	250 mL
Flour	3 cups	750 mL
Sugar	2 cups	500 mL
Baking powder	1 tsp.	5 mL
Baking soda	1 tsp.	5 mL
Salt	1 tsp.	5 mL
Buttermilk	1 cup	250 mL
Eggs	2	2
Vanilla	1 tsp.	5 mL
Sugar	3/4 cup	175 mL
Flour	1/2 cup	125 mL
Butter OR margarine	1/4 cup	60 mL

Combine strawberries and rhubarb in a saucepan. Cook over medium heat for 5 minutes until softened. Stir in lemon juice. Combine sugar and cornstarch. Slowly stir into fruit till thickened. Remove from heat and cool.

In a large bowl, beat together next 6 ingredients until crumbly. Add buttermilk, eggs and vanilla and beat until smooth. Pour 1/2 of batter in greased 9 x 13 inch (22 x 33 cm) baking pan. Spread cooled fruit on top of batter. Top with small mounds of remaining batter.

In a small bowl combine sugar, flour and butter until crumbly. Sprinkle on top of cake and bake in 350F (175C) oven for 40-45 minutes. Cool slightly before serving. Delicious!

Country Apple Crisp

Lorraine Fadden
Creston, BC

Creston, BC is known for their orchards. This apple dessert is wonderful.

Butter OR margarine	1/4 cup	60 mL
Peeled apples, sliced	4 cups	1 L
Rum, amber	1/4 cup	60 mL
White sugar	1/3 cup	75 mL
Cinnamon	1/8 tsp.	0.5 mL
Walnuts, chopped	1/2 cup	125 mL
Flour	1/2 cup	125 mL
White sugar	1/3 cup	75 mL
Salt, dash		
Butter OR margarine	1/4 cup	60 mL
Vanilla	1/2 tsp.	2 mL

In a skillet melt butter. Add apples and sauté until tender. Remove from heat and add rum. Stir in sugar and cinnamon. Put in 9 x 9 inch (22 x 22 cm) pan. Let stand for 30 minutes.

In a bowl, combine walnuts, flour, sugar and salt. Cut in butter until crumbly. Mix in vanilla. Sprinkle half over apple mixture. Bake in 400°F (205°C) oven for 15 minutes. Sprinkle remaining nut mixture on top and bake another 15 minutes. Serve with ice cream or whipped cream. Makes 4-6 servings.

Pictured on page 89.

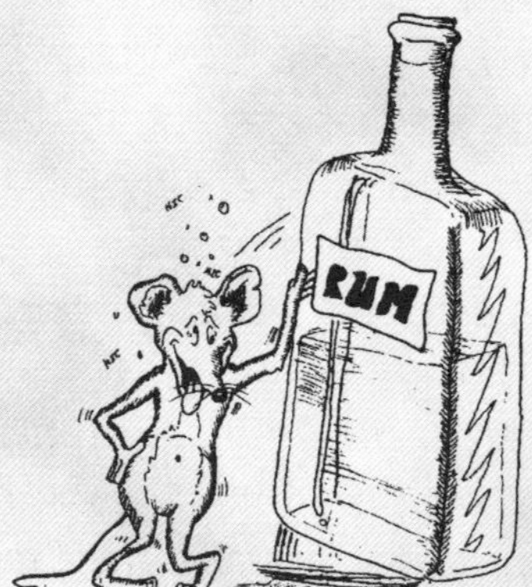

Chocolate Caramel Pecan Cheesecake

Pat and Jan Dion
Nakusp, BC

Decorate top with pecan halves for an added touch.

Vanilla wafers, crushed	3 cups	750 mL
Butter OR margarine, softened	1/2 cup	125 mL
Caramels	1 1/2 cups	375 mL
Evaporated milk	1 cup	250 mL
Pecans, chopped	1 cup	250 mL
Cream cheese, softened	2x 8 oz.	2x 250 g
Sugar	1/2 cup	125 mL
Vanilla	1 tsp.	5 mL
Eggs	2	2
Chocolate chips, melted	1/2 cup	125 mL
GLAZE:		
Chocolate chips	3/4 cup	175 mL
Butter OR margarine	2 tbsp.	30 mL
Water	2 tbsp.	30 mL

Combine vanilla crumbs and butter. Press into 9 inch (23 cm) springform pan. Bake in 350°F (175°C) oven for 10 minutes.

In a saucepan, melt caramels and evaporated milk over medium heat (can be melted in microwave). Stir and pour over crust. Sprinkle pecans on top of caramel mixture.

In a bowl, beat together next 5 ingredients. Pour over pecans and bake in 350°F (175°C) oven for 40 minutes.

GLAZE: Melt chocolate chips, butter and water together. Stir until smooth. Pour over cheesecake. Chill. Serves 16.

Pictured on page 125.

Lemon Meringue Torte

Pat and Jan Dion
Nakusp, BC

You can store this dessert in the freezer and enjoy a piece when the craving for lemon sneaks up on you.

Flour	2 cups	500 mL
Butter OR margarine	1 cup	250 mL
Baking powder	2 tsp.	10 mL
Eggs	2	2
Large egg yolks	6	6
Sweetened condensed milk	11 oz.	300 mL
Frozen lemonade OR limeade	12 oz.	355 mL
Whipping cream, whipped	2 cups	500 mL
Egg whites	6	6
Sugar	1/2 cup	125 mL

In a bowl or food processor, blend flour, butter, baking powder and eggs together. Spread into 9 x 13 inch (22 x 33 cm) baking pan. Bake in 350°F (175°C) oven for 20-30 minutes.

Beat together egg yolks, condensed milk. and lemonade. Pour half over crust. Return to oven and bake 15 minutes. Cool.

Fold whipped cream into remaining lemon mixture. Pour over cooled crust and filling.

Beat egg whites, adding sugar slowly. When stiff, spoon and spread over filling. Broil for 1 minute or till topping is lightly browned. Cover with foil or plastic wrap. Freeze. Remove from freezer 20 minutes before serving. Spoon sliced strawberries and whipped cream on top. Serves 16.

Chocolate "To Die For"

Carol Koorbatoff
Shoreacres, BC

You will be rich if given a nickel for everytime you are requested to serve this dessert.

9 x 13 chocolate cake	1	1
Chocolate pudding (NOT instant)	2x 6 oz.	2x 170 g
Coffee liqueur (optional)	2 tbsp.	30 mL
Whipped topping, thawed	2x 500 g	2x 1 L
Skor chocolate bars, crumbled	8	8

Prepare cake and pudding according to package directions. Cool. Cut cake in cubes.

In a large dessert serving bowl, assemble following layers: 1/2 cake cubes; 1/2 coffee liqueur; 1/2 chocolate pudding; 1/2 whipped topping; 1/2 chocolate bars. Repeat layers. Serves 10-12.

Variation: Substitute Skor chocolate bars with favorite chocolate bars.

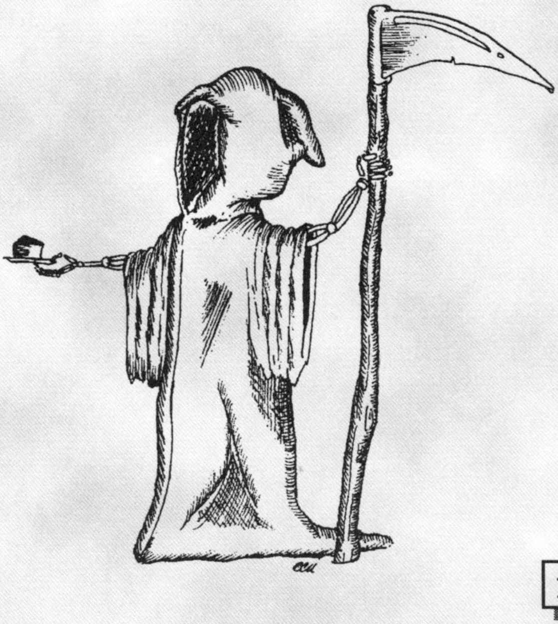

Drumstick Dessert

Lyn Arikado
Nakusp, BC

This treat can be kept in the freezer until all is eaten... if it lasts that long.

Graham wafer crumbs	2 cups	500 mL
Unsalted peanuts, finely chopped	1/3 cup	75 mL
White sugar	2 tbsp.	30 mL
Butter OR margarine, melted	1/3 cup	75 mL
Cream cheese	8 oz.	250 g
Peanut butter, smooth	1/2 cup	125 mL
White sugar	1/2 cup	125 mL
Vanilla	2 tsp.	10 mL
Whipped topping	2 cups	500 mL
Vanilla ice cream	3 1/2 cups	825 mL
Caramel sundae topping	2/3 cup	150 mL
Peanuts, chopped	1/2 cup	125 mL

In a bowl, mix together graham wafer crumbs, peanuts, sugar, and butter. Press into bottom of greased 9 x 13 inch (22 x 33 cm) pan.

In another bowl, beat cream cheese, peanut butter and sugar until smooth. Mix in vanilla and whipped topping. Add ice cream and again beat until smooth. Spread evenly onto graham wafer crust.

Drizzle half caramel topping on ice cream filling. Using knife, gently fold in caramel. Smooth top and drizzle remaining caramel on top. Sprinkle with peanuts. Cover and place in freezer for 4-6 hours before serving.

To serve: Remove from freezer, let sit at room temperature for 3-4 minutes, cut into squares and enjoy.

Huckleberry Cheesecake

Margaret MacDonald
Salmo, BC

We all look forward for the huckleberries to be in season. The Kootenay Country is loaded with these delightful berries.

Graham wafer crumbs	2 cups	500 mL
Brown sugar	1/4 cup	60 mL
Butter OR margarine, melted	1/2 cup	125 mL
Cream cheese	8 oz.	250 g
Icing sugar	3/4 cup	175 mL
Vanilla pudding, instant	5 oz.	153 g
Milk	1/2 cup	125 mL
Whipping cream, whipped	1 cup	250 mL
Water	1/2 cup	125 mL
Sugar	1/2 cup	125 mL
Huckleberries	2 cups	500 mL
Cornstarch	2 tbsp.	30 mL
Cold water	2 tbsp.	30 mL

Mix first 3 ingredients together. Press into ungreased 10 inch (25 cm) springform or 9 x 13 inch (22 x 33 cm) pan.

In a bowl, beat cream cheese and icing sugar until smooth. Set aside.

Mix pudding and milk together. Add to cream cheese mixture. Mix until well blended. Fold in whipping cream. Pour filling onto crust.

In a saucepan, bring first amount of water to a boil. Add sugar and huckleberries. Stir and simmer until fruit is softened. Mix cornstarch with remaining water. Slowly stir into huckleberries until thickened. Cool and spread on filling. Enjoy!

Apple-Nut Pudding

Elaine Gustafson
Burton, BC

Unlike regular puddings, this has a moist cake texture.

Large egg, lightly beaten	1	1
Sugar	1/2 cup	125 mL
Vanilla	1/2 tsp.	2 mL
Flour	1/2 cup	125 mL
Baking powder	1 tsp.	5 mL
Salt	1/4 tsp.	1 mL
Tart apple, chopped	1 cup	250 mL
Walnuts, finely chopped	1/4 cup	60 mL

Mix together egg, sugar and vanilla in a bowl. Add flour, baking powder, and salt. Beat well. Stir in chopped apple and walnuts. Pour in greased 8 x 8 pan (20 x 20 cm) pan. Bake in 350°F (175°C) oven for 25 to 30 minutes.

Serve with vanilla ice cream or whipped topping. Serves 6.

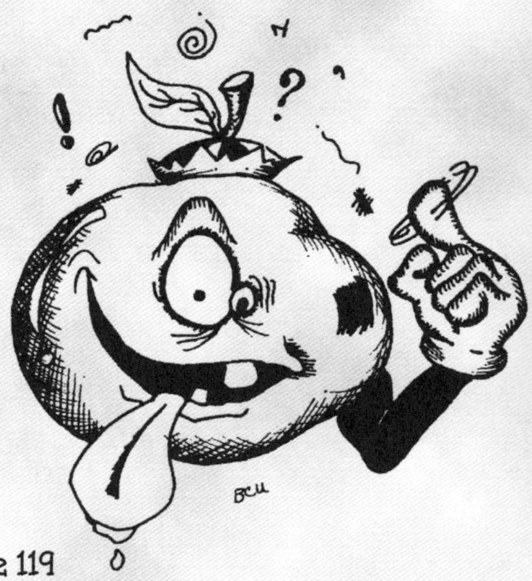

Chocolate Pecan Caramel Cheesecake, page 119
Harvest Apple Pie, page 146
Dutch Tarts, page 148

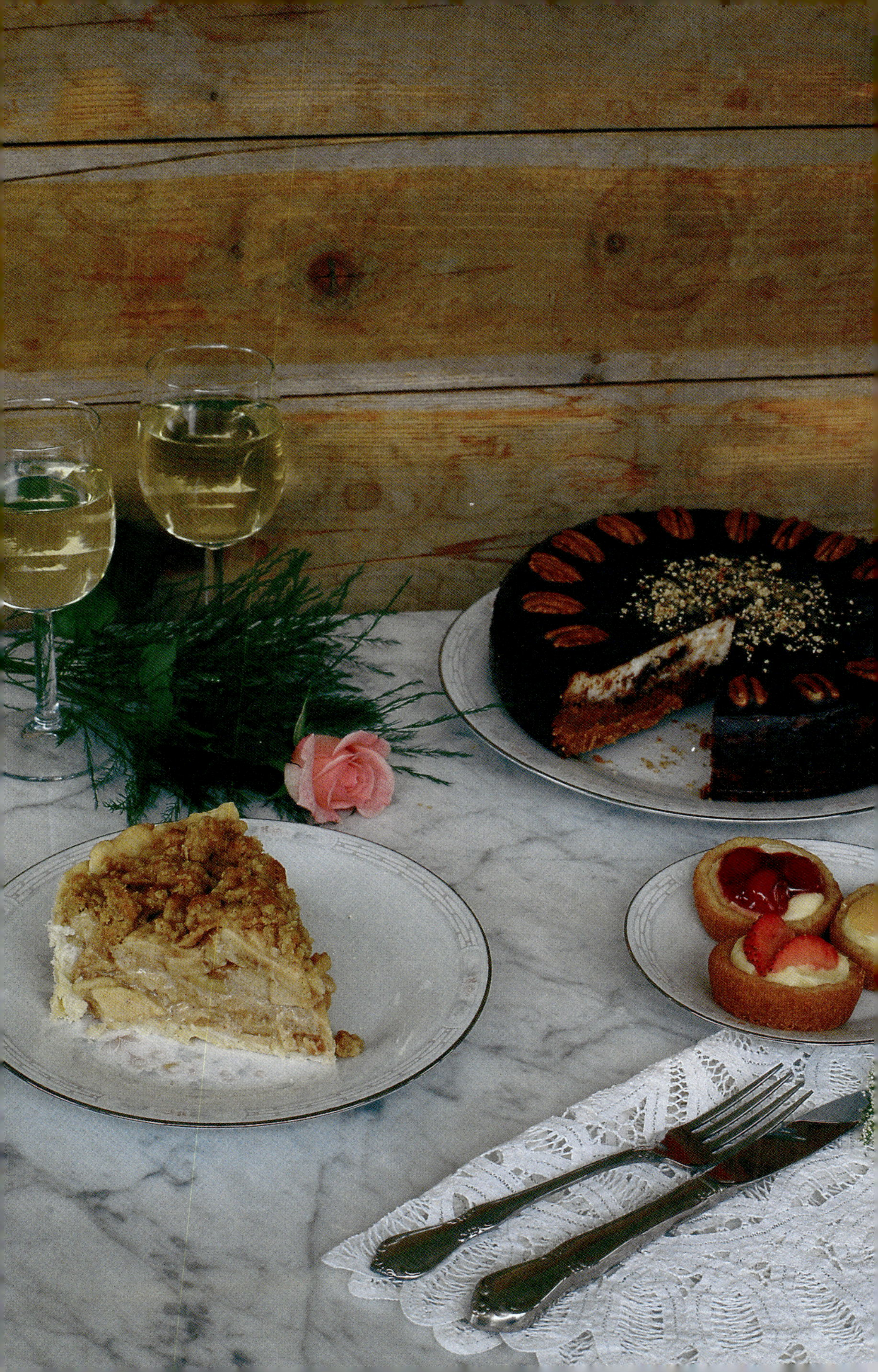

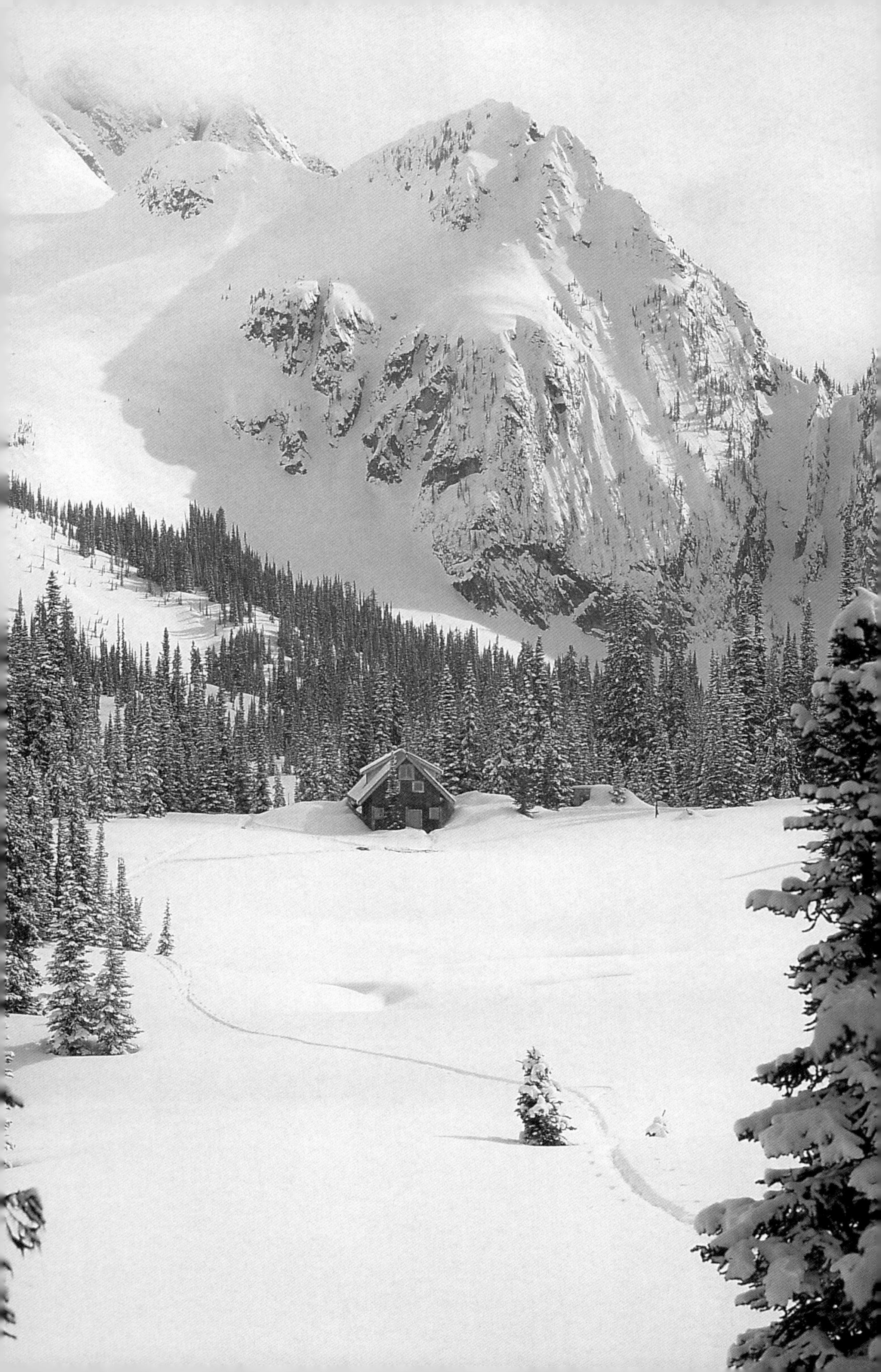

Pineapple Delight

Jean Hewat
Nakusp, BC

This square will bring you smiles of delight.

Graham cracker crumbs	2 1/2 cups	625 mL
Butter OR margarine, melted	1/2 cup	125 mL
Butter OR margarine	1/2 cup	125 mL
Icing sugar	1 1/2 cups	375 mL
Eggs	2	2
Whipping cream, fresh	1 cup	250 mL
Vanilla	1 tsp.	5 mL
Icing sugar	1 tbsp.	15 mL
Crushed pineapple, drained	19 oz.	540 mL

Mix graham crackers and butter together. Press into 9 x 13 inch (22 x 33 cm) pan. Bake in 250°F (120°C) oven for 15 minutes. Cool.

In a bowl, cream together butter and icing sugar. Add eggs and beat well. Spread over a cooled crust.

Beat together whipping cream, vanilla and icing sugar until stiff. Fold in pineapple. Spread over filling. Sprinkle extra graham wafer crumbs on top for a finishing touch. Chill. Cut into squares and serve.

Back country lodge near McKean Lakes in the Valhalla Mountains.

Flourless Cappuccino Cake With Raspberry Sauce

Geoff Hampson
Mountain Gypsy Cafe
Rossland, BC

Spoil yourself with this classy cake. Very light and moist.

Semisweet cooking chocolate, chopped	16 oz.	500 g
Unsalted butter	1 lb.	500 g
Brown sugar	1 cup	250 mL
Freshly brewed coffee, espresso preferred	1 cup	250 mL
Coffee liqueur	1 oz.	28 g
Light cream	1 cup	250 mL
Eggs, beaten	8	8
Frozen raspberries	10 oz.	284 mL

In a medium bowl, add first 5 ingredients. Place bowl over simmering water until chocolate is melted. Whisk until blended.

In a saucepan, bring cream to boil. Whisk vigorously until frothy. Pour into chocolate mixture. Whisk eggs into chocolate. Pour into parchment or grease proof paper lined 9 inch (22 cm) springform pan. Place pan into shallow tray of hot water and bake in 350°F (175°C) oven for approximately 1 hour. When tested for doneness, center of cake should be slightly moist. Cool completely before removing from pan.

Puree raspberries and force through strainer into a bowl to remove seeds. Chill. To serve, pour over cake and top with whipped cream.

Variation: Use instant espresso instead of freshly brewed coffee.

Almond Oat Cookies

June Brown
Nakusp, BC

A cookie for the almond lovers. Hide the cookie jar!

Butter OR margarine	$^2/_3$ cup	150 mL
Sugar	$^2/_3$ cup	150 mL
Rolled oats	3 cups	750 mL
Egg, beaten	1	1
Almond extract	1 tsp.	5 mL
Slivered almonds, blanched	$^2/_3$ cup	150 mL

In a bowl, cream together butter and sugar. Blend in rolled oats, egg, almond extract and almonds. Roll dough into $1^1/_2$ inch (4 cm) balls. Place on greased cookie sheet and press with fork to flatten. Bake in 375°F (190°C) oven for 10 minutes. Makes $2^1/_2$ dozen cookies.

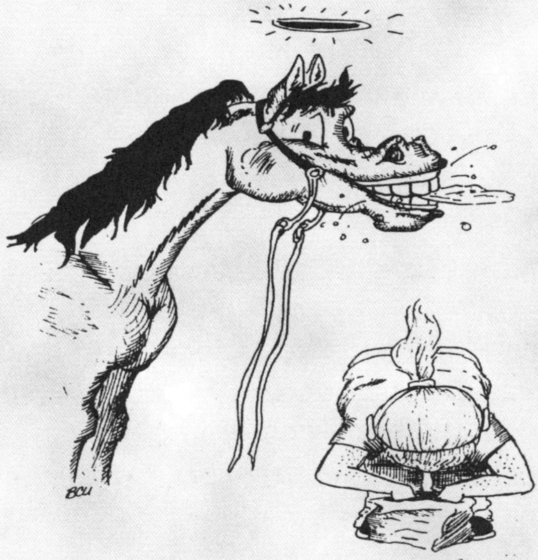

DID YOU KNOW... Kaslo is the home to the "S.S. Moyie", the world's oldest surviving passenger sternwheeler. In 1915, it was known to have carried 400 passengers.

Famous Cookies

Margaret Bateman
Nakusp, BC

"A lady was served these cookies in a restaurant and asked if she could have the recipe. She was told it would cost two fifty, so she told them to add it to her bill. What a shock when she found out it cost $250.00 - so she vowed to give the recipe to everyone."

Flour	2 cups	500 mL
Salt	1/2 tsp.	2 mL
Baking powder	1 tsp.	5 mL
Baking soda	1 tsp.	5 mL
Butter OR margarine	1 cup	250 mL
Sugar	1 cup	250 mL
Brown sugar	1 cup	250 mL
Eggs	2	2
Vanilla	1 tsp.	5 mL
Chocolate chips	2 cups	500 mL
Chopped nuts	1 1/2 cups	375 mL
Rolled oats	2 1/2 cups	625 mL

Combine flour, salt, baking powder and baking soda in bowl.

In another bowl, cream together butter and sugars. Add eggs and vanilla and beat until light and creamy. Mix in dry ingredients. Stir in chocolate chips, nuts and rolled oats. Roll into balls and press down on cookie sheet. Bake in 375°F (190°C) oven for 7-9 minutes. Makes 4-5 dozen.

Pictured on page 143.

Prize Winning Peanut Butter Cookies

Levi Dupuis
Nakusp, BC

"My Mom and I like to bake these cookies together. These cookies won first place at the 1996 Nakusp Fall Fair." Levi is 7 years old.

Whole wheat flour	1 1/4 cups	300 mL
Baking soda	1/2 tsp.	2 mL
Salt	1/4 tsp.	1 mL
Natural peanut butter	2/3 cup	150 mL
Shortening	1/2 cup	125 mL
Brown sugar	2/3 cup	150 mL
Sugar	1/4 cup	60 mL
Egg	1	1

Sift together flour, baking soda and salt in bowl.

Stir natural peanut butter before measuring. Cream together peanut butter, shortening and sugars until smooth. Beat in egg. Stir in dry ingredients until well mixed. Roll into small balls and press with floured fork on lightly greased cookie sheet. Bake in 350°F (175°C) oven for 12-15 minutes, until browned. Let cool 5 minutes before removing to cooling rack. Makes 2-3 dozen.

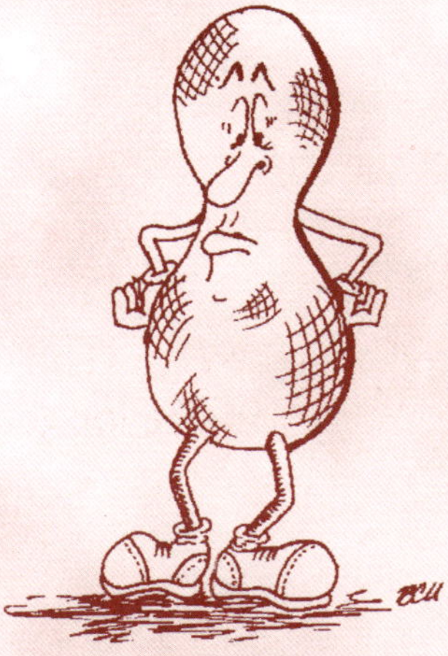

Ginger Snaps

Betsy-Ann Gallinger
Crawford Bay, BC

A mouthwatering soft ginger cookie.

Butter OR margarine	1 1/2 cups	375 mL
White sugar	2 cups	500 mL
Eggs	2	2
Molasses	1/2 cup	125 mL
Flour	4 cups	1 L
Baking soda	2 tsp.	10 mL
Cinnamon	1 tsp.	5 mL
Cloves	1 tsp.	5 mL
Ground ginger	1 tsp.	5 mL

In a large bowl, cream together first 4 ingredients till smooth.

Sift flour, baking soda and spices into creamed mixture. Beat well. Roll into balls and place on greased cookie sheet. Press with a fork dipped in water. Bake in 375°F (190°C) oven for 8 minutes. Let cool slightly before removing to cooling rack. Makes 6 dozen cookies.

Pictured on page 143.

DID YOU KNOW... The Kootenay Lake ferry from Balfour to Crawford Bay is the longest free ferry ride in the world.

Danish Butter Cookies

Bobbi Lang
Nakusp, BC

This may seem like a large batch of cookies, but this cookie dough can be refrigerated up to 3 months before using. Perfect when a freshly baked cookie is craved.

Butter OR margarine	3 cups	750 mL
Sugar	3 cups	750 mL
Flour	6 cups	750 mL
Vanilla (or almond flavoring)	3 tsp.	15 mL
Salt, pinch		
Egg yolks	3	3
Egg whites, slightly beaten	3	3

In a large bowl, mix butter, sugar, flour, vanilla and salt. Beat in egg yolks until soft dough forms. Refrigerate for 40 minutes.

Roll dough into small balls and press with fork (or cookie press) on cookie sheet. Brush lightly with egg whites. Bake in 325°F (160°C) oven for 12-15 minutes. Let cool slightly before removing to wax paper lined table.

DID YOU KNOW... Egg facts: If you shake the egg and you hear a rattle, you can be sure it's stale. A really fresh egg will sink and a stale one will float. Fresh eggs are rough and chalky in appearance. Old eggs are smooth and shiny.

Mom's Whipped Shortbread Cookies

These have been passed down as a family favorite. A traditional Christmas cookie. Thanks mom!

Butter	1 lb.	500 g
Icing sugar	1 cup	250 mL
Flour	3 cups	750 mL
Cornstarch	1 cup	250 mL
Vanilla	$1\frac{1}{2}$ tsp.	7 mL

Maraschino cherries, quartered

Beat butter until creamy in large bowl.

Sift dry ingredients together and gradually add to butter, beating well after each addition. Stir in vanilla. Roll in balls and place on greased cookie sheet. Press down with floured fork. Place cherry quarter in center of dough. Bake in 300°F (150°C) oven for 15-20 minutes. Do not let brown. Let cool slightly before removing to wax paper lined table or cooling rack. Makes 3-4 dozen cookies.

DID YOU KNOW... The largest recorded fish caught in the Kootenay Country region was a prehistoric Sturgeon which measured approximately 12 feet long and weighed over 350 lbs. In early 1997, a Canadian and possible World record for the largest Bull Trout was caught in the Kootenay Lake weighing in at $29\frac{1}{2}$ pounds.

Peanut Butter Squares

Elizabeth Strong
Winlaw, BC

If calorie conscious, only use half icing on squares.

Brown sugar	1/2 cup	125 mL
Corn syrup	1/4 cup	60 mL
Butter OR margarine	1/2 cup	125 mL
Peanut butter	1 cup	250 mL
Vanilla	1 tsp.	5 mL
Corn flakes cereal	2 cups	500 mL
Crispy rice cereal	2 cups	500 mL

ICING:

Evaporated milk	1/4 cup	60 mL
Brown sugar	1 cup	250 mL
Butter OR margarine	2 tbsp.	30 mL
Corn syrup	2 tbsp.	30 mL
Icing sugar, to thicken		

Mix brown sugar, corn syrup and butter in saucepan. Boil for 1 minute. Remove from heat and stir in peanut butter, vanilla, corn flakes cereal and crispy rice cereal. Press into greased 8 x 8 inch (20 x 20 cm) pan. Chill.

Combine evaporated milk, brown sugar, butter and corn syrup in saucepan and boil 2 minutes. Cool. Stir in icing sugar to thicken. Spread on cooled cereal mixture. Cut in small squares to serve.

DID YOU KNOW... Mayonnaise gives dry hair a good conditioning. Apply 1/2 cup (125 mL) mayonnaise to dry, unwashed hair. Cover with plastic bag and wait for 15 minutes. Rinse a few times before shampooing thoroughly.

Corn Flake Squares

A nice change from Rice Krispie Squares.

Butter OR margarine	1/2 cup	125 mL
Corn syrup	1/2 cup	125 mL
Coconut	1/2 cup	125 mL
Brown sugar	1/2 cup	125 mL
Corn flakes cereal	5 cups	1250 mL

In a large saucepan bring butter, corn syrup, coconut and brown sugar to a boil. Boil for 3 minutes stirring constantly. Add corn flakes cereal and mix well. Press into greased 8 x 8 inch (20 x 20 cm) pan. Cut into squares.

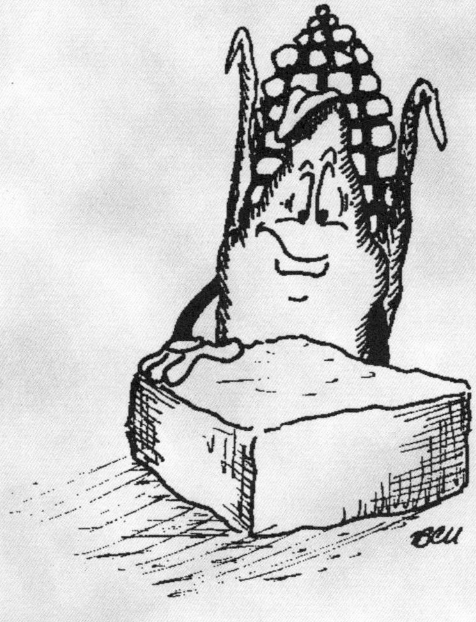

DID YOU KNOW... For rock-hard brown sugar, add a slice of bread to the package, close the bag tightly, and in a few hours the sugar will be soft again.

Butterscotch Oat Bars

Barbara Bond
Nelson, BC

"These oatbars have been passed on by my grandmother. An old family favorite."

Shortening, butter OR margarine, melted	1/2 cup	125 mL
Brown sugar, lightly packed	1 cup	250 mL
Vanilla	1 tsp.	5 mL
Rolled oats	2 cups	500 mL
Flour	1/4 cup	60 mL
Baking powder	1 tsp.	5 mL
Salt	1/2 tsp.	2 mL

In a large bowl, cream shortening, brown sugar and vanilla.

In another bowl, combine rolled oats, flour, baking powder and salt. Stir into creamed mixture. Lightly press into greased 8 x 8 inch (20 x 20 cm) square pan. Bake in 300°F (150°C) oven for 30 minutes. Remove from oven and cut into squares while still hot. Makes 16 squares.

Pictured on page 143.

DID YOU KNOW... To remove rust from tin pie pans, dip a raw potato in cleaning powder and scour.

Home Made Chocolates

Lorraine Fadden
Creston, BC

Melting chocolate squares with paraffin wax for chocolate coated candy gives you a coating that won't melt in your hands.

FILLING:

Butter OR margarine	1 cup	250 mL
Icing sugar	3 lbs.	1.5 kg
Corn syrup	2 tbsp.	30 mL
Sweetened condensed milk	14 oz.	395 mL
Vanilla	1 tsp.	5 mL

ADDITIVE OPTIONS:

Various nuts (walnuts, almonds, pecans, hazelnuts, etc.)
Various flavorings (almond, maple walnut, etc.)
Various fruits (maraschino cherries, crystallized ginger, dried fruit)

CHOCOLATE COATING:

Semi-sweet chocolate	2x 1 oz.	2x 30 g
Paraffin wax	2/3 brick	2/3 brick

FILLING:
In a bowl, cream together butter and icing sugar. Add corn syrup, condensed milk and vanilla. Mix well. Divide dough and add chosen additives. Roll into chocolate sized balls.

COATING:
Melt semi-sweet chocolate and paraffin wax together in a saucepan.

Stick a toothpick into flavored balls and dip into chocolate. Set on waxed paper. Place in refrigerator until set. Store in cool place.

Almond Roca

Bev Brennen
Beasley, BC

At Christmas, add a few chopped candied cherries for some festive color.

Graham wafers	14 oz.	400 g
Butter OR margarine,	1 cup	250 mL
Almond flakes	1 cup	250 mL
Brown sugar	3/4 cup	175 mL

Line two cookie sheets with foil. Lay out graham wafers to cover foil.

Melt butter in a medium saucepan. Add almonds and brown sugar. Bring to a boil. Immediately spread over graham crackers. Bake in a 350°F (175°C) oven for 10 minutes or until top lightly bubbles. Cool slightly. Remove from foil and cool completely on cooling racks. Store in air tight container. Freezes well.

Pictured on page 143.

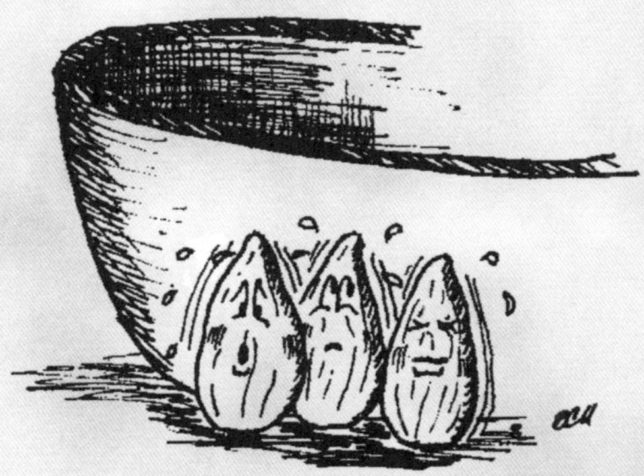

WHEW!! I don't think she saw us. Now, on "three" we run for the silverware drawer...

Candied Poppycock

Heather Strong
Winlaw, BC

This treat can also be made in the microwave.

Popped popcorn	8-10 cups	2-2.5 L
Pecans and almonds	1 cup	250 mL
Butter OR margarine	1 cup	250 mL
White sugar	1 2/3 cups	400 mL
Corn syrup	1/2 cup	125 mL
Vanilla	1 tsp.	5 mL

Mix popcorn and nuts in large bowl.

In a medium saucepan add butter, sugar and corn syrup. Heat to boiling over medium heat, stirring constantly. Boil for 5-6 minutes till mixture reaches hard-ball stage 250°F (120°C) on candy thermometer or until small amount dropped into cold water forms a hard ball. Stir in vanilla. Pour over popcorn/nut mixture. Mix well. Spread out on lightly sprayed (non stick cooking spray) sheet to cool. Store below normal room temperature. Do not store in refrigerator.

Pictured on page 143.

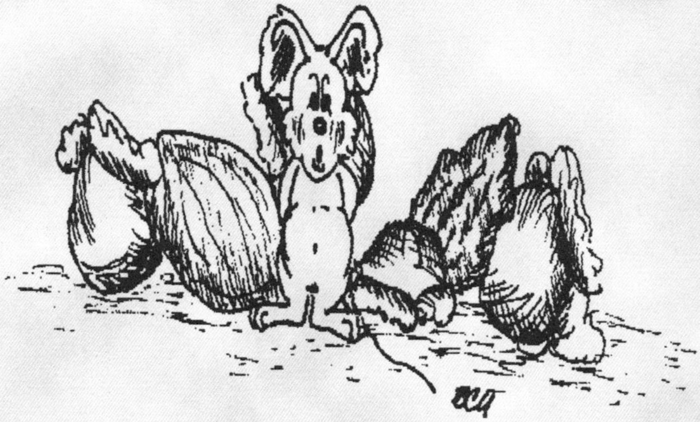

Angel Pie

Heather's Kitchen
Rock Creek, BC

Simply irresistible and heavenly. This family favorite has been in Heather's family since the turn of the century. She has been enjoying this passed down recipe for 57 years.

Large egg whites	5	5
Cream of tartar	1/2 tsp.	2 mL
Sugar	3/4 cup	175 mL
Large egg yolks	5	5
Sugar	1/2 cup	125 mL
Lemon juice	1/2 cup	125 mL
Water	1/2 cup	125 mL
Cornstarch	2 tbsp.	30 mL
Whipping cream, whipped	2 cups	500 mL

In a bowl, beat egg whites and cream of tartar until stiff. Add first amount of sugar and beat until blended. Scrape into greased 10 inch (25 cm) pie plate. Bake in 275°F (140°C) oven for approximately 45 minutes, till golden brown. Let cool.

In top half of double boiler cream together egg yolks, remaining sugar, lemon juice, water and cornstarch. Stir over boiling water until mixture thickens. Cool.

Layer meringue with whipped cream, lemon filling and top with final layer of whipped cream.

Variation: Substitute lemon juice with same quantity of any citrus juice.

Delicious Deep Dish Plum Pie

Suzanne White
Fletcher Creek
Kaslo, BC

He put in his thumb and pulled out a plum and said "what a lucky boy am I."

Unbaked, deep dish pie shell	1	1
Sugar	1 cup	250 mL
Flour	1/4 cup	60 mL
Butter OR margarine	2 tbsp.	30 mL
Pitted plums, halved (prune plums are best)	4 cups	1 L
Light cream	1/2 cup	125 mL

Prepare own pie pastry. Lap pastry over edge of pie plate.

Mix sugar, flour and butter until crumbly. Sprinkle half into pie shell.

Pack plum halves cut side down on crumbly mixture in pie shell. Drizzle cream over plums. Sprinkle remaining crumb mixture on top. Place pie on baking sheet and bake in 425°F (220°C) oven for 10 minutes. Reduce oven to 350°F (175°C) and bake another 40 minutes. Serve warm.

Variation: Substitute plums for apple/huckleberry OR apple/blackberry combinations. Use 3 cups (750 mL) of apples and 1 cup (250 mL) of berries. The berries give the pie a wonderful color.

Country Granola, page 101
Ginger Cookies, page 132
Famous Cookies, page 130
Candied Poppycock, page 140
Poppyseed Chiffon Cake, page 115
Dropped Doughnuts, page 98
Lemon Loaf, page 102
Carrot Pineapple Muffins, page 109
Cornflake Squares, page 136
Almond Rocco, page 139
Creamy Dreamy Butter Tarts, page 145
Butterscotch Oat Bars, page 137

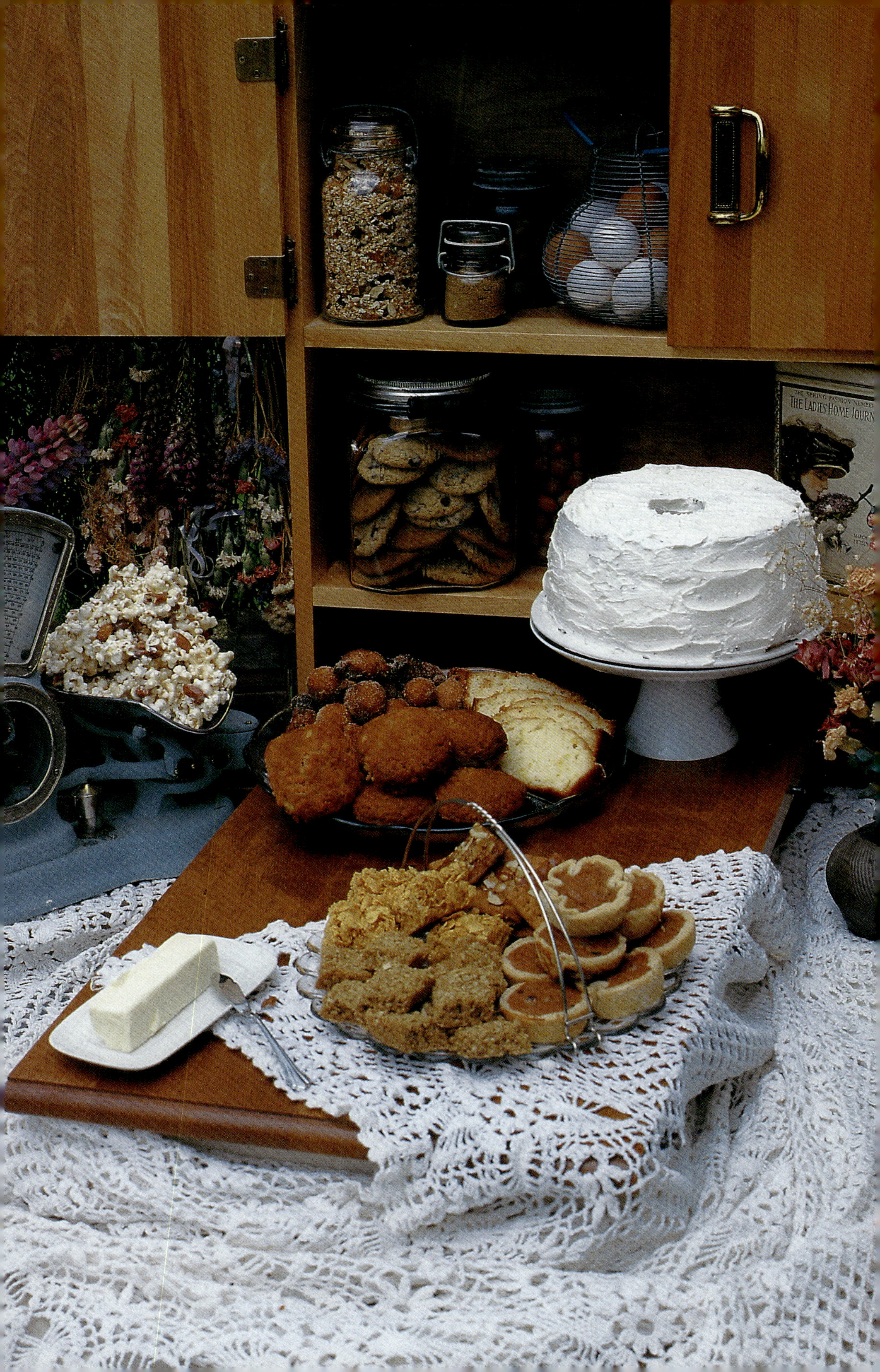
THE SPRING FASHION NUMBE
THE LADIES' HOME JOURN

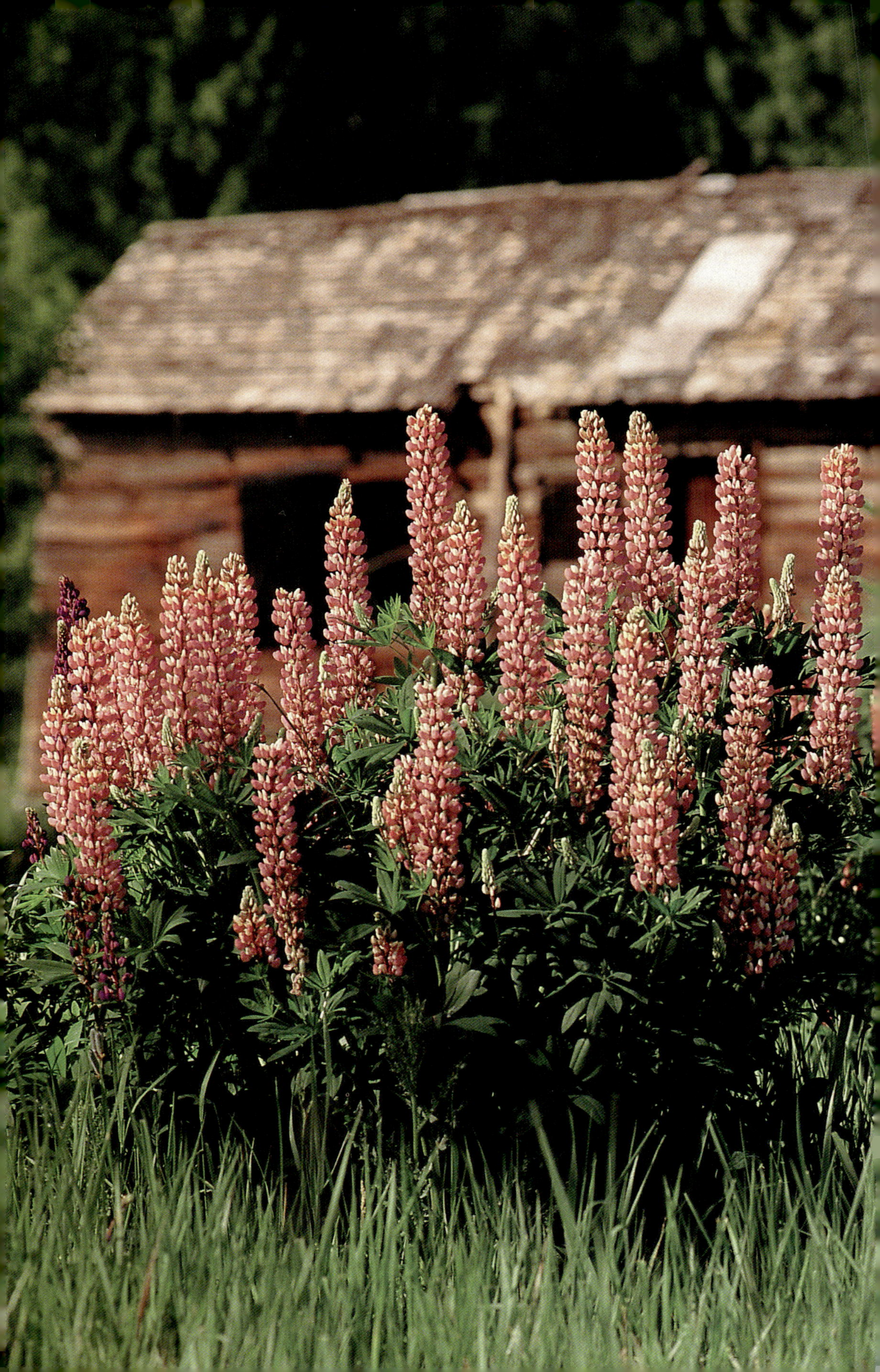

Creamy Dreamy Butter Tarts

After trying many butter tart recipes over the years, this creamy filling is my favorite.

PASTRY:		
Unbaked, tart shells	24	24
FILLING:		
Eggs	4	4
Butter OR margarine, melted	1/4 cup	60 mL
Brown sugar	2 cups	500 mL
Vanilla	1 tsp.	5 mL
Light cream	1/4 cup	60 mL
Raisins	2 cups	500 mL

Prepare own tart shells.

In a bowl beat eggs until creamy. Blend in butter, brown sugar and vanilla. Stir in cream and raisins. Fill tart shells and bake in 400°F (205°C) oven for 5 minutes. Reduce heat to 375°F (190°C) for another 12 minutes. Cool slightly before removing from pans. Freezes well. Makes 24 tarts.

Pictured on page 143.

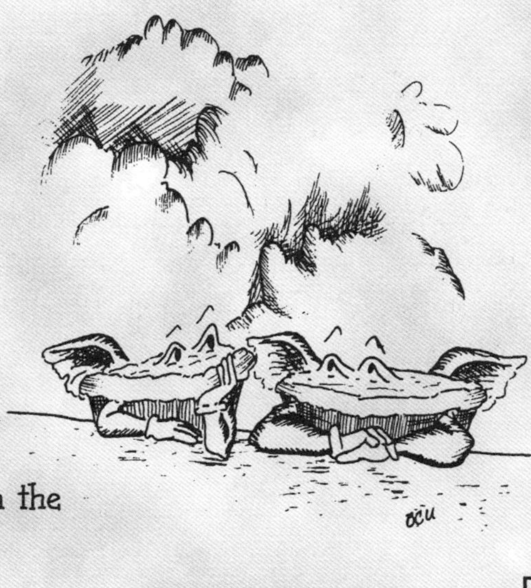

Lupins in field near rustic barn in the Fruitville area.

Harvest Apple Pie

Anne Brandt
Nelson, BC

This creamy apple pie was given 2 thumbs up by all the testers. Needless to say there were no leftovers.

Unbaked, 9" (23 cm) pie shell	1	1

FILLING:

Egg	1	1
Sour cream	1 cup	250 mL
White sugar	3/4 cup	175 mL
Flour	2 tbsp.	30 mL
Cinnamon	1 tsp.	5 mL
Apples, peeled and thinly sliced	3 cups	750 mL

TOPPING:

Flour	1/2 cup	125 mL
Brown sugar	1/2 cup	125 mL
Rolled oats	1/2 cup	125 mL
Butter OR margarine	1/2 cup	125 mL

Prepare own pie pastry.

Beat together egg, sour cream, sugar, flour and cinnamon in a large bowl. Stir in apples. Scrape into pie shell.

In a separate bowl, mix flour, brown sugar, rolled oats and butter until crumbly. Sprinkle evenly over apples. Pat down slightly. Bake in 425°F (220°C) oven for first 10 minutes. Reduce heat to 350°F (175°C) and bake for another 35 minutes. Let stand 20 minutes before serving.

Pictured on page 125.

Bumbleberry Pie

Sandra Scott
Nakusp, BC

For those that have trouble choosing between berry pies, here is the solution... a combination.

Unbaked, 9" (23 cm) pie shells	2	2
Apples, peeled and chopped	2 cups	500 mL
Blackberries	1 cup	250 mL
Raspberries	1 cup	250 mL
Rhubarb, chopped	1 cup	250 mL
Sugar	3/4 cup	175 mL
Flour	4 tsp.	20 mL
Cornstarch	4 tsp.	20 mL
Butter OR margarine	4 tsp.	20 mL
Lemon juice	1 tbsp.	15 mL

Prepare own pie pastry.

In large bowl combine apples, blackberries, raspberries and rhubarb.

Mix together sugar, flour and cornstarch. Toss in with fruit to cover evenly. Transfer to unbaked pie shell. Dot fruit with butter and sprinkle lemon juice on top. Cover with top crust and seal. Bake in 425°F (220°C) oven for 15 minutes. Reduce heat to 350°F (175°C) and bake another 35 minutes or until golden brown and bubbly.

Pictured on page 71.

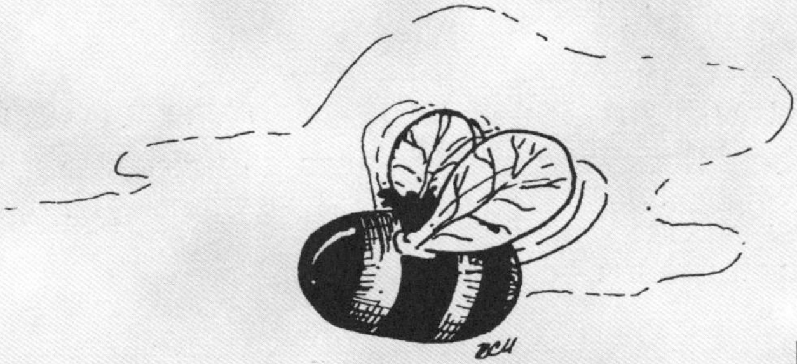

Dutch Tarts

Sylvia Bowins
Creston, BC

Flour	2 cups	500 mL
White sugar	2/3 cup	150 mL
Brown sugar	2/3 cup	150 mL
Baking powder	1/2 tsp.	2 mL
Baking soda	1/2 tsp.	2 mL
Butter OR margarine	1 cup	250 mL
Egg, beaten	1	1

In a bowl, mix together flour, sugars, baking powder and soda. Beat in butter and egg until smooth. Divide dough into 36 one inch (2.5 cm) balls. Press each into tart or muffin tins to form small shell. Bake in 375°F (190°C) oven for 6-8 minutes. Cool slightly before removing from pans. Fill with fruit, pudding or desired filling and top with whipped topping. Makes 24 shells.

Pictured on page 125.

Chocolate Shortbread Crust

Lyn Arikado
Nakusp, BC

A universal crust which can be used with your favorite filling.

Flour	1 cup	250 mL
Butter OR margarine	1/2 cup	125 mL
Icing sugar	2 tbsp.	30 mL
Semi-sweet chocolate, melted	1 oz.	30 g

In bowl mix together flour, butter and icing sugar. Blend in chocolate. Spread in bottom and sides of 9 inch (23 cm) pie pan. Chill for 30 minutes before baking. Bake in 425°F (220°C) oven for 10 minutes. Cool before using.

Rhubarb Ginger Jam

Elaine Gustafson
Burton, B.C.

"Ginger grows wild here, in the form of a vine. I gather it in the spring, chop it and freeze it for cooking as well as jam. DEE-LISHUS!"

Rhubarb, thinly sliced	3 cups	750 mL
Prepared ginger	1/2 cup	125 mL
Water	3/4 cup	175 mL
Sugar	5 1/2 cups	1375 mL
Liquid pectin	3 oz.	85 g

Combine rhubarb, ginger and water in large pot. Cover and simmer for 1 hour, until fruit is soft.

Measure 3 cups of rhubarb mixture into separate large pot. Add sugar. Mix well. Cook on high heat to full boil. Hard boil 1 minute. Remove from heat and stir in pectin. Continue to stir for 5 minutes, skimming foam off top of fruit. Pour into hot sterilized jars. Cover with 1/8 inch (3 mm) hot paraffin. Makes 3 half pints.

Variation: The prepared ginger indicated in this recipe uses the local wild ginger vine, cut into 1/4 inch (6 mm) pieces. It may be substituted with 1/2 cup (125 mL) crystallized ginger.

DID YOU KNOW... "Nikkei Internment Memorial Centre" in New Denver is the only site in Canada dedicated to tell the story of Japanese Canadians during World War II.

Jalapeño Pepper Jelly

Lyn Arikado
Nakusp, BC

A wonderful jelly that compliments crackers with the garlic spread on page 14.

Seeded, chopped green peppers	3	3
Seeded, chopped jalapeño peppers	1/4-1/2 cup	60-125 mL
White vinegar	1 1/2 cups	375 mL
Granulated sugar	6 1/2 cups	1.5 L
Liquid pectin	6 oz.	170 mL
Drops of green food coloring (optional)	4-6	4-6

Combine green peppers, jalapeño peppers and vinegar in blender. Blend until finely chopped. Pour into large pot.

Add sugar. Heat on medium, stirring constantly until boils.

Stir in pectin. Increase heat to high and return to a full rolling boil. Hard boil for 5 minutes, stirring constantly. Remove from heat and let sit 1 minute. Skim off foam.

If desired, add food coloring. Pour into hot sterilized jars to within 1/4 inch (6 mm) of top. Seal. Makes 10-12 jelly jars.

Pictured on page 17.

DID YOU KNOW... Greenwood is the smallest incorporated city in Canada with a present population of approximately 850 people.

Sweet Pepper Jelly

Marilyn Massey
Nakusp, BC

"This is excellent with meats."

Sweet red peppers, chopped	12	12
Lemon, chopped	1	1
Peaches, chopped	2	2
Pears , chopped	3	3
Vinegar	varies	
Sugar	varies	

Put red peppers, lemon, peaches and pears in a large pot. Cover with vinegar and let stand for 2 days.

Measure 1 cup sugar to every 1 cup pulp into a separate large pot. Bring to a boil. Reduce heat and simmer to a jelly consistency. Pour into hot sterilized jars to within 1/4 inch (6 mm) of top. Seal.

Whipped Raspberry Jam

Elizabeth Strong
Perry Siding
Winlaw, BC

"Excellent color and no certo!"

Raspberries, packed	6 cups	1.5 L
Sugar	6 cups	1.5 L

In a large pot, bring raspberries and sugar to a boil. Boil for 3 minutes. Remove from heat, place pot in sink and beat for 6 minutes. Pour into hot sterilized jars and seal with 1/8 inch (3 mm) hot paraffin. Makes 5 half pints.

Pictured on page 107.

Dandelion Jelly

Sylvia Bowins
Creston, BC

"The best time to make this jelly is the first growing and blooming of the dandelions. Tastes almost like a honey kind of jelly."

Water	4 cups	1 L
Dandelion tops, washed	4 cups	1 L
Lemon juice	1 tbsp.	15 mL
Pectin crystals (certo)	2 oz.	57 g
White sugar	4 cups	1 L

In a large pot, boil water and dandelion tops for 5 minutes.

Strain 3 cups (750 mL) dandelion liquid into another pot. In same pot, stir in lemon juice and pectin crystals. Bring to a boil. Add sugar and boil for another $1\frac{1}{2}$ minutes. Let sit for 5 minutes. Pour into hot sterilized jars within $\frac{1}{2}$ inch (6 mm) of top. Seal. Makes 4 half pints.

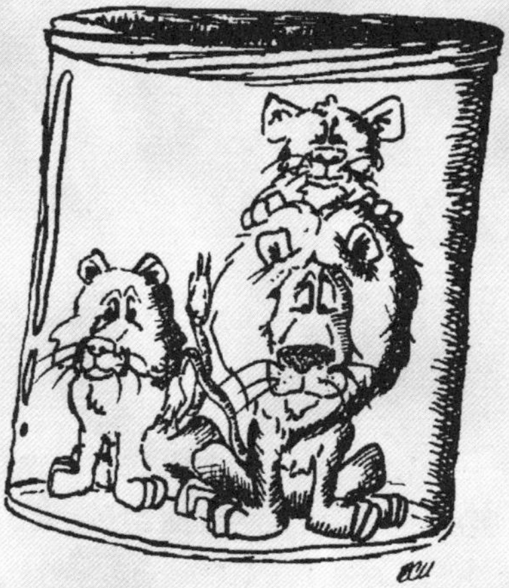

DID YOU KNOW... On an average, dandelion greens contain far more vitamin A than spinach or any other garden vegetable.

Pickles in a Bucket

Elizabeth Strong
Perry Siding
Winlaw, BC

A pickle recipe that requires no cooking. "Keeps in fridge indefinitely. This recipe was passed down from my sisters in Saskatchewan."

Cucumbers, thinly sliced	6-7 lbs.	2.5-3 kg
Large onions, sliced	2	2
Green peppers, sliced	2	2
Red pepper, sliced (optional)	1	1
White sugar	4 cups	1 L
White vinegar	2 cups	500 mL
Coarse (pickling) salt	2 tbsp.	30 mL
Turmeric	1 tsp.	5 mL
Celery seed	1 tsp.	5 mL
Mustard seed	1 tsp.	5 mL

Fill a 4-quart (4 L) ice-cream bucket with thinly sliced cucumbers, onions and peppers. Mix well.

In a large bowl, mix together remaining 6 ingredients (do not heat). Pour over cucumbers. Cover and store in refrigerator. More cucumbers may be added the next day. Ready to eat in 3 days.

Pictured on page 71.

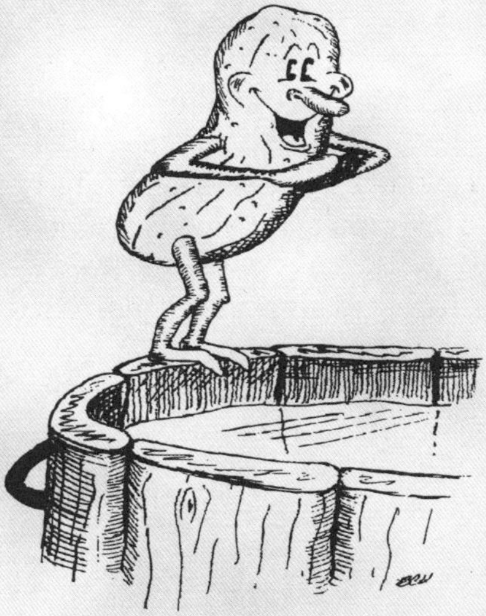

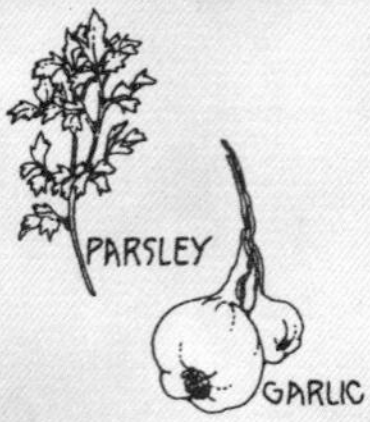

HERBS AND SPICES GUIDE

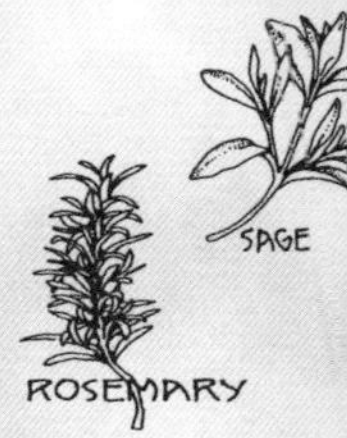

Herbs are the leaves of annual or perennial shrubs.
Spices are derived from the bark, roots, fruits or berries of perennial plants.

Many fresh herbs and spices are grown throughout the Kootenay Region. These various herbs and spices are used for food, medicine, scent, and flavoring. This guide is to assist you with matching these herbs and spices with food. To substitute fresh herbs for dried, use approximately three times more of the snipped fresh herb.

Allspice: soups, stews, pot roasts, meat loafs, hams, fish, vegetables, cakes, fruit pies, candy, frostings.

Anise: beef, pork, beets, carrots, cakes, cookies, pastries.

Basil: meats, poultry, fish, soups, stews, pasta, vegetables, stuffing, salads, dressings, sauces, dips, eggs.

Bay leaf: soups, stews, pot roasts, fish, eggs, potatoes, rice, salads, gravies.

Caraway seed: pot roasts, meat loaves, soups, stews, eggs, stuffing, salads, vegetables, sauerkraut, breads, dips, sauces.

Cardamom: meats, poultry, fish, fruit salads, dressings, pastries, breads, cookies, cakes.

Cayenne pepper: Mexican and Italian, dishes, dressings, curry dishes, eggs.

Celery (seed,flakes, salt): meats, poultry, stews, soups, salads, breads, stuffing, sauces, spreads, relishes, vegetable juices.

Chervil: meats, poultry, fish, eggs, vegetables, salads, dressings.

Chili powder: meat loaf, hamburgers, shrimp, poultry, Mexican dishes, soups, stews, eggs, vegetables, cheese sauces, gravy, French dressing, spreads.

Chives: cheese dishes, sauces, eggs, vegetables.

Cinnamon: pork, poultry, lamb, beef stews, soups, vegetables, fruit salads, salad dressings, breads, pies, cakes, puddings, cookies, beverages.

Cilantro: Mexican dishes, dips

Cloves: corned beef, pork, lamb, fish, poultry, baked beans, soups, tomato sauces, vegetables, dressings, relishes, breads, fruit salads, cakes, cookies, pies.

Coriander: pork, poultry, soups, stews, curries, stuffing, fruit salads.

Cumin: Mexican, Spanish and Chinese dishes, cheese dishes, stews, soups, salad dressings, vegetable dips.

Curry powder: meats, poultry, fish, soups, vegetables, salad dressings, dips, cheese spreads, relishes.

Dill(weed, seed): meats, lamb, poultry, fish, seafood, soups, stews, vegetables, salads, dressings, breads, eggs, dips, sauces, spreads.

Fennel: meats, poultry, fish, seafood, stews, vegetables, soups, salads, dressings, pickles.
Garlic (clove, salt, powder): meats, poultry, stews, vegetables, casseroles, soups, dressings, sauces, marinades, dips, spreads, pickles.
Ginger: meats, poultry, seafood, soups, oriental dishes, vegetables, dressings, cakes, cookies, pies, fruits, pickles.
Mace: meat loaf, poultry, veal, fish, seafood, soups, fondues, vegetables, fruit, cakes, breads, cookies.
Marjoram: meats, poultry, fish, soups, stews, vegetables, dressings, salads, eggs, fruits, sauces.
Mint: lamb, poultry, fish, vegetables, salads, fruits, sauces, marinades, desserts, beverages.
Mustard (dry, seed): corned beef, sauerkraut, eggs, macaroni salads, dressings, marinades, sauces, dips, pickles.
Nutmeg: meat loaves, meatballs, poultry, seafood, vegetables, quiches, fruits, sweet salad dressings, eggnog, breads, cakes, cookies, pies, custards.
Oregano: meats, poultry, veal, fish, seafood, stews, soups, casseroles, pasta dishes, vegetables, eggs, sauces, dips.
Paprika: meats, fish, soups, stews, eggs, potatoes, sauces.
Parsley: meats, poultry, fish, casseroles, soups, salads, vegetables, sauces, breads, garnish.
Pepper: meats, poultry, fish, casseroles, soups, salads, vegetables, marinades.
Poppy seed: pasta, breads, desserts.
Red Pepper (ground, crushed): Mexican and Cajun dishes, eggs, dips, spreads, cream soups, French dressing.
Rosemary: meats, poultry, fish, soups, stews, casseroles, vegetables, salads, eggs, breads.
Saffron: poultry, fish, seafood, rice, breads, cakes.
Sage: meats, poultry, fish, soups, stews, casseroles, vegetables, stuffing, sauces, gravies, eggs, breads, pastries, beverages.
Savory: meats, poultry, fish, stews, soups, vegetables, sauces, eggs.
Sesame seed: poultry, fish, stir fry dishes, vegetables, marinating sauces, breads, cookies.
Tarragon: meats, poultry, fish, seafood, soups, stews, casseroles, vegetables, salads, cheese dishes, eggs, dressings, sauces.
Thyme: meats, poultry, meat loaves, meatballs, fish, seafood, soups, stews, casseroles, vegetables, salads, eggs, breads, sauces.
Turmeric: poultry, fish, soups, eggs, salad dressings, sauces, relishes, pickles.

Other:

EDIBLE WEEDS & PLANTS

BERRIES:

Black Raspberries, Wild Currants, Thimbleberries, Elderberries, High Bush Cranberries, Wild Blueberries/Strawberries, Huckleberries and Salal Berries- Many of these listed berries used for jams, jellies, syrups, pies and/or muffins.

Bearberry-Also known as "Kinnickinnick". Cook and serve cold.

Juniper Berries- Used for flavoring cordials, vinegars, soups, stews and venison.

Oregon Grape- A cross between huckleberry and black currant in taste. Use for jelly as an accompaniment to meat.

BRACKEN FERN: Was once known as edible however, even at fiddlehead stage, bracken plants contain carcinogenic substances. They are no longer recommended as edible.

CHICKWEED: Cut stems with leaves and flowers and use raw in salads or simmer in minimum of water, adding butter and salt after cooking.

CHICORY: Leaves resemble those of dandelion and flowers are large and showy, resembling daisies but lacking yellow centre. Dry and ground roots for an excellent coffee substitute. Young leaves can be eaten raw in salads or cooked in two changes in water.

CLOVER: Red and white clovers young leaves and flowers may be used raw in salads. They are wholesome and very nutritious. Use flowers in herbal tea.

DANDELION: Use young leaves as salad greens, cooked as a vegetable or used for jelly. Roots that are dried, roasted and ground may be used as a coffee substitute.

FIREWEED: Use young leaves as cooked vegetable, young shoots as raw vegetable.

LAMBS QUARTERS: Also known as "Pigweed". Young leaves and tops used as salad ingredient or may be cooked as greens. Can be cooked to a mush, dried, and ground into flour or used in soups and stews. Full of vitamins and minerals.

MILKWEED: Only use young shoots, very young leaves, and half-matured green seedpods as cooked vegetable (changing the water twice). Flowers, dried and crumbled, can be used as replacement for brown sugar, being rich in nectar.

MINERS LETTUCE: Can be eaten raw as a salad green, or cooked like spinach.

NETTLE: Use as cooked green (do not overcook). Are very nutritious, being a good source of vitamins A and C and some minerals.

PONDEROSA PINE: Also known as "Western Yellow Pine". Seeds have pleasant flavor. Can be added to muffins, breads and buns.

PURSLANE: This plant is richer in iron than any other leafy vegetable except parsley. Is also rich in vitamin A. Cook in sauces or used chopped in salads. Suitable for pickling and a good substitute for cucumber; using your favorite pickle recipe. Seeds can be boiled and eaten as porridge. Ground seeds into meal, and mixed in equal parts with flour to make bread or muffins.

ROSE HIPS: Use for jellies, jams or syrup. Rich in vitamin C.

SHEEP SORREL: Also known as "Sourgrass". Use young leaves raw in salads. Can be used for making soups and sauces, as a seasoning for fish, pork, veal, lentils, rice, or potatoes. It is rich in vitamin C.

WILD GINGER VINE: A mild ginger flavor used in vinegar or as ginger substitute.

Many weeds are both edible and palatable. However, a few weedy species can be dangerous to eat, as they are capable of causing illness or death to animals and humans. Those that attempt to utilize weeds as food should always be positive in identifications by being able to identify the poisonous species, should exercise extreme caution in selecting plants for the table and prepare edible weeds properly. Avoid roadside weeds or berries due to possible sprays and exhaust fumes.

INDEX

A Great Gift Idea!

Order...

"Kootenay Country Kitchens Cookbook... a collection of Kootenay Favorites" at $21.95 per book plus $2.00 per copy for shipping and handling.

_______ Copies of "Kootenay Country Kitchen Cookbook" at $21.95

_______ Plus $2.00 per copy for shipping & handling.

_______ Subtotal

_______ Plus GST (subtotal x .07) Canada Only

$_______ Enclosed (U.S. orders - please pay in U.S. funds)

Name ____________________

Street ____________________

City ____________________

Province ____________ Postal Code ________

Make cheque or money order payable to:
"KOOTENAY KITCHENS PUBLISHING"
Box 656, Nakusp, British Columbia, Canada V0G 1R0